HELP!

IT'S

DANGEROUS
OUT HERE

HOW TO WALK IN
SUPERNATURAL PROTECTION

Vikki Burke

Help! It's Dangerous Out Here – How to Walk in Supernatural Protection
ISBN 978-1-8920026-34-9
© 2019 by Vikki Burke
P.O. Box 150043
Arlington, TX 76015

Published by Vikki Burke
P.O. Box 150043
Arlington, TX 76015

Cover Design: Michael Saltar
Text Design/Layout: Lisa Simpson

CONTENTS

PERILOUS TIMES

Grabbing a heart-shaped valentine from his locker, a shy teen passed it to a girl before blushing as he hurried to class. Girls giggled, lockers slammed and love was in the air as cards, candy and balloons passed from student to student. Teachers worked to get their attention back on history, calculus and diagramming sentences. Arriving by Uber, 19-year-old Nikolas Cruz opened his bag and pulled out an assault rifle. Going from room to room, he fired into classrooms, leaving 17 dead.

Five months earlier, Cruz had posted these chilling words on a YouTube channel. "I'm going to be a professional school shooter."

Why Cruz chose Valentine's Day to launch his murderous career at Marjory Stoneman Douglas High School in Parkland, Florida, remains a mystery. Maybe he'd heard of the infamous St. Valentine's Day massacre carried out by Al Capone's mob on February 14, 1929. Maybe not. Maybe

Nikolas Cruz just enjoyed the irony of killing kids on the holiday associated with love.

Either way, the two Valentine's Day massacres are stark reminders that violent crimes aren't new.

What *is* new though is their increased frequency, and who's committing them. Modern mobsters aren't the only ones making headlines. It's all kinds of people, from teenagers to terrorists:

- The guy next door building a bomb in his spare bedroom or driving a rental truck into bikers and pedestrians on a path in New York City.

- Religious extremists turning an Ariana Grande concert in England into a killing field or shooting a priest in France in a church during mass.

- Children killing their families.

- A husband murdering his pregnant wife and children.

Seemingly ordinary people committing hate crimes, acts of road rage, and rapes.

Add to the list the contemporary dangers posed by new strains of viruses and antibiotic-resistant bacteria, and economic threats posed by large-scale computer hacking, identity theft, and unstable world markets, and it's no wonder that chronic anxiety has become a major world problem.

Without a doubt, we're living in dangerous days.

We're seeing come to pass all around us what the Apostle Paul warned us about in the Bible. He said in Second Timothy 3 that "in the last days perilous times will come."[1] The Greek word translated *perilous* means *dangerous, harsh, fierce, savage and hard to bear, difficult or stressful.*

Then Paul defined the characteristics that will prevail during these days:

People will be lovers of themselves, lovers of money, boastful, proud, abusive, disobedient to their parents, ungrateful, unholy, without love, unforgiving, slanderous, without self-control, brutal, not lovers of the good, treacherous, rash, conceited, lovers of pleasure rather than lovers of God—having a form of godliness but denying its power.[2]

Without love. Those two words speak volumes. Perhaps that was the message intended by the Valentine's Day massacres. *I will kill you on Valentine's Day, because I am…without love.*

How the world needs Jesus.

Days That Try Men's Souls

Thomas Paine, confronted with the dangers of the Revolutionary war, wrote these words to encourage a frightened nation facing battle: "These are the days that try men's souls. The summer soldier and the sunshine patriot will, in this crisis, shrink from the service of their country; but he that stands it now, deserves the love and thanks of man and woman."

Today, Christians need to hear something similar. In these soul-trying times we need to be reminded that in this crisis the casual Christian and the powerless pew warmer will shrink from the service of their God. But he who stands in faith now will live in victory.

We may not be crossing the Delaware with George Washington or fighting to the death for our independence like the patriots Paine addressed, but right now the Church faces the same questions: How will we respond to the perils that confront us? Will we trust God to preserve us? What can we expect from Him?

A lot of Christians don't know how to answer those questions. They're not sure what they can expect from God. They believe the old saying, *You never really know what God is going to do*. So, they respond to danger the same way people do who don't know God—in fear and defeat.

In the Bible, however, we see something entirely different. We see that God always does what He says He'll do. That He's not a liar. He keeps the promises He made in His written Word. We don't see in the Scriptures Old Testament Jews or early Christians cowering in fear. We see them facing down danger with courage, trusting God's promises of protection, and coming out victorious—even in the face of the most impossible odds.

Take Daniel, for instance. When he heard the edict from King Darius that any person who prayed to anyone except the king for the next 30 days would be thrown in the lion's den, Daniel boldly and fearlessly kept praying to God. He didn't shrink back in fear or beg for mercy. He didn't ask for an exception. He didn't even hide in a cave and do his praying in secret.

Three times a day, Daniel opened his window, threw back the curtains, and prayed loud enough for the neighbors to hear. As a result, he was thrown in the lion's den. He spent a whole night there. But when the king came to check on him the next morning, he was still alive. God had shut the lion's mouth! When he came out, there were no wounds found on him.

Daniel's three friends, Shadrach, Meshach and Abednego had a similar story. When they were told to either bow to the 90-foot tall golden image of Nebuchadnezzar or be burned in the fiery furnace, they made a bold choice. They stood their ground, refused to bow to the idol, and worshipped God.

They didn't try to negotiate a deal with King Nebuchadnezzar. They didn't cower and come up with a compromise. They just trusted God.

Their boldness enraged Nebuchadnezzar, so the king prepared to throw them into the flaming furnace. He ordered the oven to be heated seven times hotter than normal and the three defiant Jews to be bound and thrown into the flames. After they were tossed in, however, the king saw an astonishing sight. Another man who looked like the Son of God joined Shadrach, Meshach, and Abednego and walked with them in the flames.

What happened? Jesus showed up in the fiery furnace and they suffered no harm!

King Nebuchadnezzar called out to the three men, and they walked out of the fire. Their bodies weren't burned, their hair wasn't singed, and they didn't even smell like smoke.

Facing the Giant

Then, of course, there was David. You've heard about him. Goliath was terrorizing Israel's army with threats so terrifying that even Israel's king was shivering with fear. Yet David, a young teenager, boldly squared off against the giant. He went out to fight him without armor or even a sword. He *ran* at Goliath, carrying only a slingshot and five smooth stones, screaming:

> You come against me with sword and spear and javelin, but I come against you in the name of the LORD Almighty, the God of the armies of Israel, whom you have defied. This day *the LORD* will deliver you into my hands, and I'll strike you down and cut off your head. This very day I will give the carcasses of the Philistine army to the birds and the wild animals, and the whole world will know that there is a God in Israel. All those gathered here will know that it is not by sword or spear

that the LORD saves; for the battle is the LORD's, and he will give all of you into our hands.[3]

Those weren't just idle threats David was yelling either. He followed his words with action. He did what he said, killed the giant, and cut off his head. Then he led Israel's army against the Philistines all the way to Goliath's hometown, slaughtering them along the way.

How, as such a young boy, was he able to do it?

He understood God's promises of protection. He knew beyond a doubt that God was not only with him but empowered him.

A Better Covenant

These are all miracles of protection from the Old Testament. But because of the death, burial and resurrection of Jesus, as Christians, we have a better covenant then even the Old Testament heroes.[4] A covenant based on better promises. The covenant that's ours today!

The Apostle Peter demonstrated the power of this new covenant when he was arrested, thrown in prison, and sentenced to die. He didn't weep or wail. He didn't beg or fall into depression.

So, how did he respond to his potentially deadly situation?

He put his faith in Jesus and went to sleep. Although he was bound between two soldiers, he slept soundly. During the night, a light shone in his cell. An angel awakened him and led him out of the prison to safety.

The Apostle Paul showed the same courage when he was bitten by a viper on the island of Malta. As he gathered brushwood in the whipping wind and freezing rain a snake latched onto his hand and injected its deadly venom, yet Paul showed no alarm at all. He didn't call for help. He didn't ask for first aid. He didn't even gather a group for prayer.

Certain of God's protection he just shook the snake off into the fire and went about his business. The islanders waited to see him die, but he suffered no ill effects.

Covenant Confidence

The Bible is filled with such exploits. It recounts one situation after another about men and women who faced death without fear. What made them so brave?

They put their trust in God's Covenant of protection.

Many people these days are unfamiliar with the term covenant. If you're like I was when I first became a Christian, you may not even know what the word means.

In its simplest form, a covenant is a binding agreement between two parties. It's a contract that's been signed by the individuals involved and filed in court. God's Covenants are what He promises to do for people if they believe and obey Him.

In Genesis, for instance, God made a covenant with Abraham. He told Abraham that if he would go to a land the Lord would show him, He would make his descendants into a great nation. He also promised to protect him saying, "I will bless those who bless you and curse those who treat you with contempt."[5]

Those were some remarkable covenant promises, given Abraham's situation!

He was 75 years of age and his wife was barren. He was about to leave the security of his home and family and go to a foreign and possibly unfriendly land. But he believed God's covenant promises anyway. Despite the feebleness of his own body and his wife's dead womb, he trusted God to give him descendants—and when he was 99 years old the impossible came to pass. And Abraham had a son named Isaac.

Abraham showed the same confidence in God's promise of protection. When his nephew Lot was taken captive by a band of armed men, he got his servants together and went to rescue him. Never mind that Abraham's little group was seriously outnumbered. Never mind that he had to fight several kings and their combined armies to set Lot free. Abraham took on those armies in battle and won. He whipped them completely and took back everything they'd stolen—people, goods and livestock.

How could Abraham, with only 318 servants, defeat thousands of professional soldiers? His covenant with God included protection, and he knew it.

God's Covenant with Noah

Look back a little further in Genesis and you'll find that Noah also had a covenant with God that included protection. At that time, wickedness had become so great on earth that the Lord regretted making man. God warned Noah what was coming and told him what to do. Then He sent a worldwide flood to destroy the earth and everything evil living on it, except Noah and his family.

Noah believed God and obeyed Him. He built the ark according to God's instructions and for years he preached to people about the coming doom, and the mercy God would have on those who would repent. Sadly though, they didn't listen. They continued in their wicked ways. Noah didn't win a single convert. The only people who believed him were his sons and their families.

Eventually, time ran out, and along with his family Noah entered the ark. When he did, Genesis 7:16 says, "the Lord shut him in." What a tremendous sense of safety and comfort that phrase carries! Shut in by God in that place of security, when judgment covered the earth, Noah remained unharmed. The rising flood tides lifted him heavenward, above the raging water. Outside the ark, the world was being destroyed. Inside was peace, safety and provision.

What God did for Noah and his family is a beautiful picture for those of us who are in Christ today. It points to the supernatural protection that's been provided to us through the power of the New Covenant.

Think about it! Daniel, Shadrach, Meshach, Abednego, David, Peter and Paul—all born into Old Covenant homes—understood God's covenant promises. What would happen if we and our families had that same understanding today? How would it affect the way we face danger?

The answer is clear. It would make us as bold and brave as our scriptural forefathers were. It would empower us, even in these perilous times, to live free of fear in the ark of God's promises of protection.

WINNING WITH SPIRITUAL WEAPONS

Terry Mize couldn't believe what he was hearing. Sure, he'd known there would be hardships when he moved his family to Guadalajara, Mexico, to work with a missionary center there. But not what this missionary described. "It's not just being eaten by bugs or getting sick from spoiled food," the man explained. "We may be off preaching in a village somewhere when a drunk stumbles up and shoots us."

"I don't know what page of the missionary handbook you read, but you didn't get that out of the Word of God," Terry said. "If somebody shoots me, who have I helped? If I leave my wife and family in Guadalajara and drive into the mountains to preach and nobody knows where I am when I get shot, who have I helped?

"My family would never see me again. They would be left not knowing what happened to me. I sure didn't help them. I didn't help the village. The people who heard me preach would decide that what I preached didn't work. I didn't help the guy who shot me. All I did was let him add murder to his problems. What you're saying is just a cop-out. All I'd be doing was taking a one-way journey to heaven without helping anyone. If some guy pulls a gun on me, I'll pull the Word of God on him!"

Terry knew the kind of talk that missionary was spewing could rob a him of his faith. He'd had enough; he wouldn't listen to more. He'd gone to Houston to pick up an organ and a sound system someone had donated to the ministry. Now he had to drive almost a thousand miles to get it back to Guadalajara. After getting the equipment across the border, he spent the night in Zacatecas.

The next morning as he left town, he listened to a recording of Kenneth Copeland preaching on The Integrity of the Word. Seeing a hitchhiker alongside the road, he stopped and picked him up, intending to tell him about Jesus. Gathering the Spanish words he needed to witness to the man, Terry turned to look at him.

The hitchhiker pointed a gun at him.

"I'm going to kill you!" the man screamed. In one fluid motion, he stuck the gun in Terry's ribs. With the other hand, he grabbed his collar and screamed it again. "I'm going to kill you!"

Taking Authority

Terry felt his heart jump into his throat as fear gripped him. He knew that fear was more dangerous than the gun. That was the first issue he had to deal with. "God has not given me a spirit of fear," Terry announced, "but of love and power and a sound mind. So fear, get out of here in the name of Jesus. I'm not tolerating you."

Once he'd dispatched fear, Terry knew he needed to deal with the other faith killer: *mental assent*. It would get him dead, fast. Although it looks like faith, mental assent is an imposter. Christians who rely on it claim to believe God's Word, then follow it with a *but*. "Sure, I believe that we are healed by Jesus' stripes, *but* I have this pain. I know that Christ meets all my needs by His riches in glory, *but* my checking account is empty." They agree with God's Word in their minds, but not in their hearts where true faith resides.

Terry couldn't afford to make that mistake in this situation. He had to believe without a doubt that God would do what He said. He had to do just what he'd told that missionary he would do in these exact circumstances: pull the Word of God on the man with the gun.

Terry continued to drive as the hitchhiker screamed, "I'm going to kill you!"

"You can't do that," Terry replied in Spanish. "I'm a man of God. I have authority over you in the name of Jesus. You can't kill me. In fact, you can't harm me in any way."

The hitchhiker didn't understand. By all outward appearances, the one with the gun had both the power and the authority. "I rebuke you in the name of Jesus," Terry said in Spanish. He repeated it in English. Then he reminded God that according to Isaiah 54:17, no weapon formed against him would prosper. Then he quoted verses from Psalm 91.

Not by Might or by Power

Terry's mind circled scenes from television where a guy in his position slammed on the brakes and grabbed the gun. If he'd been filling his mind with TV, he might have been tempted to try it. Since he'd been filling up on God's Word, however, he knew better than to rely on his own strength. The power to save him would come from the realm of the Spirit.

"I'm a minister," Terry explained to the hitchhiker in Spanish. He didn't know what that was.

"I'm a preacher," he said. The hitchhiker knew nothing about preachers.

"I'm a priest," Terry said, thinking he might understand the concept of a man of God. It didn't impress the hitchhiker.

"I'm going to kill you," the man repeated.

"You can't kill me," Terry countered.

Speaking in English to God Terry said, "Jesus said that I have authority over all the power of the enemy. He said that nothing—*NOTHING!*—would hurt me. So, Lord, if he pulls that trigger, it's my job to believe your Word is true. It's your job to do something about the bullet. You don't have much room to work with, since the barrel is against my ribs."

The hitchhiker grew angrier each time Terry refuted what he said. Whenever the devil brought negative thoughts to his mind, Terry pulled on his left ear and told himself, "Terry, you just say what the Word of God says. Handle this in the Spirit."

"Aren't you afraid?" the hitchhiker asked, shoving the gun further into Terry's side, the hammer cocked and his finger on the trigger.

"Why should I be afraid? All you've got is a loaded gun. I've got the name of Jesus."

No Weapon Formed

The hitchhiker picked up a microphone from the equipment Terry was taking to Guadalajara. "Put that down," Terry said, "it belongs to God. Everything in this car belongs to God. I belong to God. The car belongs to God. You can't have any of it."

"Pull over into that cornfield on the side of the road," the furious man demanded. Terry pulled over and stopped. The hitchhiker grabbed the keys out of the ignition. "Get out!" he screamed.

Both men got out. "Go to the front of the car!" the hitch-hiker shouted. "Now give me your money, your watch, your rings and sunglasses. Put it all on the ground and then back up."

Terry did as he was told. The hitchhiker picked them up. Terry stuck a finger in the man's face and said, "I rebuke you in the name of Jesus Christ of Nazareth."

"Shut up!" he shouted, sticking the gun between Terry's eyes, hammer still cocked, finger on the trigger. "If you say one more word, I'll kill you!"

Terry stuck his finger in the man's face again and said, "I rebuke you in the name of Jesus Christ of Nazareth! You can't kill me or hurt me in any way!"

Crazed with anger, the man took a step back…and fired five times.

When the shots stopped, Terry took a deep breath and checked himself. He wasn't hurt. No pain. No blood. He was still alive and breathing. He still stood leaning against his car. How had he missed at such close range?

All five bullets landed between his feet.

The hitchhiker looked shocked…then puzzled. Reloading his gun, he said, "Start walking."

The Greater One

Terry walked into the cornfield saying, "Greater is He who is in me than he who is in the world. The Word of God works. I have authority over the enemy!"

Walking about 150 yards into the cornfield, the hitchhiker ordered Terry to undress. He didn't feel like a mighty man of God standing in a cornfield in his underwear, but he was alive. It seemed to Terry that when the man realized he couldn't kill him, he'd decided to rob him. He took Terry's clothes and car keys as he turned to walk back to the car. He intended to drive away.

"God," Terry said, "I've done what your Word says to do. I've operated by the Word and not in the flesh. I've taken authority. Either your Word works, or it doesn't. If it doesn't, I'm not going to pay any attention to it anymore. I'll throw it away. But I believe it works. It has kept me from being killed. I say he can't rob me either. He has every intention of getting into my car and…"

When the hitchhiker was about 20 yards from the car Terry said, "God, this isn't one of those times when I need an answer day after tomorrow. I need an answer right now!"

Terry yelled at the man, "I charge you in the name of Jesus to come back here!"

The man never broke his stride as he made a 180 degree turn and came back to where Terry stood. He threw Terry's clothes to him and said, "Put them on." As Terry put his clothes back on, the man said, "What did you want to talk to me about?"

"I don't want to talk to you about anything else except this. I'm telling you that I'm a man of God. You've found out that you can't rob or kill me. I'm going home. If you want to go with me, I'll help you in any way possible. But we aren't playing your game anymore."

"You know," the hitchhiker said shaking his head, "I like you." He stuck his gun in his belt and said, "I'm going to put my confidence in you."

Give the Devil no Place

Back at the car, he took his gun out again and said, "I'm going to drive. You sit in back."

"No!" Terry said. "I'm a man of God and I have authority over you. You can't do anything because I have all the authority in Jesus' name. This is my car and I'm going to drive. You can go or you can stay here. Now, give me my keys in Jesus' name."

The hitchhiker handed Terry his keys and they drove off. As he drove, Terry explained to the man that Jesus came and died for his sins, was resurrected for him, and was sitting at the right hand of the Father praying for him.

When they reached Jalpa, a little town halfway between Zacatecas and Guadalajara, the hitchhiker said, "I can't go with you to Guadalajara. Take me up into the mountains. I have friends in the Sierras."

Terry agreed to the detour. As they turned to go into the mountains, they saw three policemen leaning against a car in front of a police station. Pulling his gun, the man warned, "Don't do anything or I will kill you first and then kill as many policemen as I can before they kill me."

Terry turned to him looking perplexed. "What do I need them for? I've got the name of Jesus."

"Oh, yeah," he said, putting the gun away.

Parting Ways

They drove 30 miles up the mountain before Terry stopped. "Look, I can't take you any further. I have just enough gas to get to Guadalajara. All I have in cash is $2.00, but I'll give you that. You can either get out or go home with me."

"I'll get out."

Terry gave him some food he'd bought in Houston. The hitchhiker reached into his pockets and pulled out Terry's watch, rings and everything he'd tried to steal. "You can have that stuff," Terry said. "Just give me my wedding ring."

"You're giving all this to me?" the man asked with wide eyes.

"You can't steal it from me, but I can give it to you," Terry explained. "Before you get going, I want to pray for you."

Terry prayed for the man and told him where to find him in Guadalajara if he needed help. The hitchhiker walked up the mountain and Terry drove home.

"I'm sure the hitchhiker sat on the mountain and wondered why he wasn't a rich man," Terry Mize says. "The equipment I had with me was worth thousands of dollars in the United States. It was worth three times that in Mexico. If he could have stolen it, he would have been a wealthy man.

"The gun is supposed to represent power and authority in the world's system. But the authority of God's Word is more powerful. If not, those five bullets would have done me in, and the buzzards would have picked my bones out there in the cornfield."

The Weapons of God

It takes great faith in God's Word to stay in peace when someone holds a loaded gun between your eyes. Yet, faith in God was so palpable in Terry Mize's situation that he didn't jump or run when shots were fired at him.

How is that possible?

Was this a one-time miracle of God?

No, He'd do the same miracle for anybody who will stand in faith and use their authority.

Today our battle has already been settled before we ever step into the fight. Although we all face challenges that come to shake our faith, we really do have every reason to hope and believe that each trial we go through is going to turn out all right for us as we put our trust in God and follow the guidance of His Word and the leading of His Spirit.

Terry conquered in his circumstances because he used God's weaponry instead of leaning on his own wisdom. The very idea of conquering implies a conflict or battle. It's true that great victories come as a result of great conflict. We see person after person in the Bible who faced impossible odds yet overcame them.

We have been given spiritual weapons to wield God's power through prayer and faith in His Word. We can be powerful, conquering, and fearless, no matter the threat! That kind of strength isn't automatic or accidental. It is the result of intentionally and diligently taking a confident position of faith in God's Word and seeing our own ability in the light of who we are now as believers.

Each of us already has the inner substance to remain steady and unshakable. But we will only walk in the reality of that inner strength as we set our faith on God's power and His faithfulness to perform His promises. And we have to stay constant in that determined faith, even in the midst of the challenge we're facing. We have the choice to deliberately and consistently exercise our authority over fear regarding the current threat. As we do, we position ourselves to receive our own miracle, just like Terry did in Guadalajara.

What spiritual weapons did Terry apply to receive his miracle?

Weapon #1 – Faith in God's Word

The facts about your current situation may be overwhelming, but facts can be changed by the truth—God's Word is truth. The current situation you're in is subject to change. It's a lie to think your current situation is permanent. The truth is, everything is subject to change when we use faith in God's Word.

For example, when God told Abraham that he would have a child, not only was he too old, but Sarah was barren. Yet despite the odds, he believed that what God had promised He would perform.

Abraham refused to consider his own body or Sarah's barrenness. His impossible situation didn't cause him to falter but instead he grew stronger. He was absolutely convinced God was not only able but willing to do whatever He said. He never wavered when it came to believing God's promise.

How did Abraham do that? He believed that the God Who raises the dead could do the impossible. The scripture says he called those things which do not exist as though they did, and expected God to fulfill it.

This is one of the most vital aspects to understanding how faith works. Paul describes the attitude of faith saying, "So we don't look at the troubles we can see now; rather we fix our gaze on things that cannot be seen. For the things we see now will soon be gone, but the things we cannot see will last forever." [6]

What does that mean? It means we refuse to accept our current circumstances as final. But instead focus on what God has said in His Word about them. Faith always speaks the desired end result instead of the present situation.

Faith is a spiritual force that works from your heart not your mind. There is no power available to us when we only believe with our minds. *Knowing* what the Bible says is not the same as *believing* what it says. You can't reach God through your mind.

Don't be discouraged if you don't feel your faith is as strong as Abraham's was. You can develop your faith from little faith into great faith. Jesus said that faith the size of a mustard seed can move mountains. [7]

Faith grows as we meditate in God's Word daily. Romans 10:17 tells us, "faith comes by hearing, and hearing by the word of God." [8] Begin a steady diet of God's Word and it will feed your heart and cause your faith to grow.

Weapon #2 – The Believer's Authority

After the resurrection, Jesus met with His disciples saying, "All authority has been given to Me in heaven and on earth. Go therefore…."[9] When Jesus conquered death, hell and the grave He attained all authority, and then gave it to His church.

It's as though He gave us power of attorney to use His authority. I particularly like the Phillips translation of Matthew 18:18. It says, "Whatever you forbid upon earth will be what is forbidden in Heaven, and whatever you permit on earth will be what is permitted in Heaven." Because Jesus gave us His very own authority, when we speak God's Word in faith over any situation, Heaven backs what we say.

We see this authority from the very beginning in God's original plan for mankind. In Genesis 1:28, God gave us the assignment to have dominion and subdue the earth. We can either do nothing and allow the devil to wreak havoc in our lives—or we can forbid the attacks of Satan and turn the situation around.

So start right now using your God-given authority by speaking to the problem rather than about the problem.

Weapon #3 – The Name of Jesus

In speaking of the finished work of Jesus, the Apostle Paul says, "God elevated him to the place of highest honor and gave him the name above all other names, that at the name of Jesus every knee should bow, in heaven and on earth and under the earth."[10]

Think about it, everything has a name. Diseases have names. Lack is a name. Unemployment is a name. Depression is a name, and the list goes on and on.

When the Name of Jesus is spoken from the mouth of a believer, all heaven stands at attention. There is no name more powerful on earth than the Name of Jesus. No matter what we face, we can speak God's Word in that Name and it must bow!

This was first demonstrated when Peter and John went to the temple where a crippled man asked them for a handout. Peter answered saying, "I don't have money, but I'll give you this—by the power of the name of Jesus Christ of Nazareth, stand up and walk!"[11] From the beginning of the church the ability to see miracles was exhibited by using the Name of Jesus.

Terry Mize knew something that many believers have overlooked or never even considered: There is power in the Name of Jesus—and He has given us the right to use His name! The same supernatural power can work through your faith-filled words! The Name of Jesus really will change things!

Weapon #4 – Speak the Word

In the ministry of Jesus there is a clear example of how power is released through the spoken word. When a Roman centurion asked Jesus to heal his servant, Jesus agreed to go home with the soldier and heal his servant. Then the centurion said something startling:

> "Lord," the officer said, "I am not worthy to have you come into my home. Just say the word from where you are, and my servant will be healed. I know this because I am under the authority of my superior officers, and I have authority over my soldiers. I only need to say, 'Go,' and they go; or 'Come,' and they come. And to my slaves, 'Do this,' they do it."[12]

The centurion understood the power of a spoken word. He also recognized the authority Jesus held over disease. He knew that if Jesus spoke to this disease, the servant would be healed. And the centurion was right. Jesus did exactly what the soldier asked of Him, and the servant was healed that very hour.

When Jesus first heard what this soldier said, He marveled. Wouldn't you like Jesus to marvel over something you said in faith? Then Jesus said, "I haven't seen faith like this in all Israel!"[13]

This man's faith was the greatest Jesus had seen among the religious leaders of the land or even among His own disciples. He understood the force of faith, the authority of Jesus, and the power of His spoken Word.

When we find God's will in the Bible and speak it ourselves in faith, something is activated. God's power for change goes to work. Paul said:

We have the same Spirit of faith that is described in the Scriptures when it says, "First I believed, then I spoke in faith." So we also first believe then speak in faith. [14]

There is power in our words! When we choose to fill our words with God's Word, we can be confident that His power is activated on our behalf. Too often people undermine the power of God's will by continuing to talk the problem and not the solution. God's Word in your mouth is the solution.

The anointing of God that is activated with your words has the capacity to turn around any situation that needs to come into alignment with God's will! So often we face situations or conditions that need to be changed by the power of God and nothing else will do the job.

Your words can turn the direction of your business, your family, your health, and your finances.

A Different System

Today it is faith in God's Word that will change our circumstances. Faith will say what God says in every situation. Our answers rest only in the stability of our relationship with God, in the certainty of His promises, and in our capacity to hold fast to our faith in what He has said in His Word. It always comes back to this core issue: *In what do we actually place our faith?*

There's no doubt about it—these are crucial times we're living in. It's a rollercoaster ride for those whose sense of security is governed by the current news or the latest reports. But despite the current tide of events, believers can ride on top of the stormy waters that threaten to engulf the lives of so many in the world.

We are tied to a different system. While the political realm influences the world we live in, politicians don't make decisions that have the final say that determines the outcome of our lives. The economy may be struggling but God has called us to live by an economic system of giving and receiving.

When trouble comes knocking at your door, you can answer that knock with God's Word, just like Terry Mize did. You can fix your heart and mind on the promises of God and believe that what He has promised, He will perform. You can allow the Word to do its job and use it as a spiritual weapon to win every war.

SURROUNDED WITH NO WAY OUT!

Albania, Allen Shook

Gunfire rattled the window as Allen Shook peered out to see a tank lumbering down the once quiet streets. Anarchy. There was no other name for such violence and utter disregard for the law. In the six years he'd ministered in Albania, Allen had never seen anything like it.

It was March 1997, and he'd watched—astounded—as Albania imploded. The government had lost any semblance of control. The military had deserted their posts, leaving 50-caliber machine guns, rifles, tanks, mortars and hand grenades to be pillaged. The streets resounded with gunfire as teenagers played with their plunder. Even the police hauled away food, pots, pans, ammunition and anything else in sight.

In Albania, with a ministry team of five, Allen realized they were in trouble.

The events that had brought him to this place had been set in motion before he was born. In 1912, his wife's grandfather had escaped Albania and entered the United States through Ellis Island at the tender age of 14. Years later, Jesus had spoken to the immigrant's nine-year-old granddaughter, Beverly. "You will take the Gospel to Albania," He said.

When Allen and Beverly married, they'd known that Albania was the primary call of God on their lives. But initially, getting into the country appeared impossible. Following World War II, its borders had been closed. Much like North Korea today, it had become one of the worst communist countries in the world.

For years Allen had taught other believers, "If you do what they did in Bible days, you'll get Bible results." On January 1, 1991, he'd been watching football when the Lord had repeated those words back to him. *"If you go like they went in Bible days, you'll get Bible results,"* He said.

Time to Go

Allen knew the Lord was telling him it was time for him and Beverly to answer the call to Albania, but how? No American had been in or out of the country in years. And it was very, very dangerous.

The next day, Allen called the United Nations. They had no representative to Albania. However, they gave him the name and number of an Albanian woman who lived in the US and had government ties. Her husband was in Albania trying to get permission for Americans to enter the country. Behind the scenes, communism was crumbling there.

Allen and Beverly were approved to make their first trip to the country in July, 1991. Before they left, Allen went to Bartlesville, Oklahoma, to the offices of Voice of the Martyr to visit with Pastor Richard Wurmbrand and his wife Sabrina. The couple had been imprisoned and tortured for their faith in Romania.

Pastor Wurmbrand was anything but encouraging. "I'm going to do everything I can to stop you from going to Albania," he said. "It's that bad."

Unable to dissuade them, he gave them what could well be their death warrant. A duffle bag filled with Christian literature that had been translated into Albanian. Where they were going, being in possession of a Christian symbol brought a death sentence. As did every piece of paper in that duffle bag.

Allen and Beverly made out a new will, kissed their six children goodbye, and set out on their mission. Those first six weeks, and every trip to Albania since, had been marked by miracles. Signs. Wonders.

On their first trip, Allen and Beverly attended a government meeting. Following the meeting, Allen had asked to use the microphone. Taking the microphone, Allen preached the Gospel, telling everyone where they were staying, so if anyone wanted to know more about God they knew where to find them. People had flocked to them.

Miracles

On one occasion, Allen prayed for a little boy with crossed eyes. At five o'clock the next morning, someone banged on their door. It was the boy's mother. An interpreter translated her words.

"My son was blind," she said. "Now he can see. There are three cripples in the next village. Will you pray for them?"

Allen and Beverly went to the village. Inside a mud hut sat three grown men, crippled since birth. Allen told them about all the cripples from the Bible who had walked after Jesus prayed for them. When he prayed, all three men were healed. Each time Allen went back to visit, the men were still well—working on the family farm.

During another meeting, someone brought them an 18-year-old girl who was deformed. One foot was withered and her leg was the size of an arm. Her arm was twisted up her back. Her hand rested on the back of her head. When Allen saw her, compassion overwhelmed him.

He closed his eyes to pray.

"Open your eyes," the Lord said. *"I want to show you something."*

Allen opened his eyes. As he prayed, he watched both of her arms stretch out in front of her—completely well. Weeping, he looked down to see that she was standing on two perfect legs.

On another visit back to that area, Allen and Beverly bought the young woman a new pair of shoes. For the first time in her life, she needed them.

Miracles had marked each trip to Albania. Until now.

No Way Out

The ground shook as a mortar exploded nearby.

"Pack up and get out," the Lord said.

Willing and eager to obey, Allen wondered how exactly he was to do so. The airport had closed. The US Embassy couldn't be evacuated because people fired at the rescue helicopters. Roads were blocked by angry mobs with weapons.

At this point, it looked as if there was literally no way out.

Texas, Vikki Burke

I'd been attending a prayer group for several months, but as we gathered to pray that day, I realized something was different. We'd been divided into small groups. Each group had a leader and a prayer assignment. Our group was assigned to pray for Allen Shook who would be preaching in Albania that very week. We were told only the leader of the group would pray, the rest of us were to support what she prayed.

Our group leader prayed that many would receive the Lord as Allen preached the Word. She prayed for healings. For signs, wonders and miracles. As the group prayed for those wonderful things, I felt troubled and a deep sense of heaviness settled inside me.

I did my best to follow the direction our leader was praying but I couldn't deny the warning I sensed in my heart, so I silently prayed in the Spirit.

"Vikki," the leader asked with piercing blue eyes, "do you have something to pray?"

"Yes," I said. I began to use the authority Jesus had given us and prayed for the lives of Allen and his team according to Matthew 18:18-19. I forbid Satan to harm them and prayed the Holy Spirit would provide a way of escape. That *nothing* by any means would injure them. I pled the blood of Jesus over him and those with him. I declared Allen and his team would live and not die and return safely to their families!

When I opened my eyes the people in our group were staring at me. As well they should. It was quite a contrast from what our leader had been praying.

Albania, Allen Shook

Allen and the rest of his team crowded into a Ford van. Praying in the Spirit, he steered the vehicle through the streets. With all their normal escape routes closed, their only hope was to make it across the country and over the border into Greece.

Multiplied thousands of people flooded the streets, shooting weapons and robbing people at gunpoint. Looking to his right, Allen gasped. Men in a pickup had a 50-caliber machine gun aimed at them.

One twitch of a finger and they were dead.

The men swiveled the gun and fired in another direction.

The journey was slow and treacherous. Halfway up a mountain, thieves had stopped a bus and were robbing people at gunpoint. Perspiration dotted Allen's forehead. The road was so narrow that they couldn't get by unless the bandits allowed them to pass.

"Grab that towel and wrap it around your head!" the Lord ordered. *"Hold your staff out of the window so they think it's a gun and you're one of them."*

Allen wrapped the towel around his head and waved his staff out the window. The thieves waved them through.

Reaching the border, Allen realized the customs building had been ransacked and was on fire. Leaning on his horn, he sped across the border into Greece.

They were the last vehicle to escape into Greece before the border closed.

Texas, Vikki Burke

Six years after Allen's escape from Albania, his son married my daughter. I'd had no idea in 1997 I was praying for my daughter's future father-in-law. It wasn't until 2012, at the birth of our grandson Lucas that I asked Allen, "Did I ever tell you about the time I prayed for your safety in Albania?" That was the first time we'd compared notes.

The God-Protected

Knowing that God desires to provide us with protection is the first step to receiving it. Allen Shook *knew* God's Covenant promises. He also knew the powerful promise God gave us for these perilous times in First John 5:18. "The God-begotten are also the God-protected. The Evil One can't lay a hand on them."[15]

Like Allen, you're God-protected. He has taken you under His own personal care to protect you from any attack. Although such attacks may come, God has promised they won't harm you. He has you covered. The enemy can't lay a hand on you.

Jesus made this comforting declaration from the *Amplified Bible*, "I have told you these things, so that in Me you may have [perfect] peace and confidence. In the world you have tribulation and trials and distress and frustration; but be of good cheer [take courage; be confident, certain, undaunted]! For I have overcome the world. [I have deprived it of power to harm you and have conquered it for you.]"[16]

Keep that in mind the next time you hear a report that tries to frighten you. You're protected by God Himself from every attack, whether it comes from the outside or from the inside. You're in His care.

King David experienced this supernatural protection time after time and in many ways. In Psalm 121, he gives a powerful picture of it. "I will lift up my eyes to the hills—From whence comes my help? My help comes from the Lord, Who made heaven and earth."[17]

David understood, the hills and mountains surrounding Jerusalem weren't what protected the city. *The God* of the city was its Protector. In the same way, your help doesn't come from your natural surroundings, but from *the One* who always surrounds you with His love and power.

Keep and Preserve

The remainder of Psalm 121 centers around a Hebrew word for protection that describes *a guard or a hedge that is built around something*. It's the word used in Genesis 2:15 that says God put man in the Garden of Eden to dress and to *keep* it, or in other words to guard and protect it from intrusion.

In Psalm 121, this word is translated two different ways: *keep* and *preserve*. We find the first translation in verses 3 through 6: "He will not allow your foot to be moved; He who *keeps* you will not slumber. Behold, He who *keeps* Israel shall neither slumber nor sleep. The Lord is your *keeper*; The Lord is your shade at your right hand. The sun shall not strike you by day, nor the moon by night." [18]

Verses 7 and 8, however, use the second translation. "The Lord shall *preserve* you from all evil; He shall *preserve* your soul. The Lord shall *preserve* your going out and your coming in from this time forth, and even forevermore."

Six times we're told that God will keep or preserve us. Six times in just that one psalm God said He would place a hedge around you to protect you from all evil; to protect your soul (which includes your mind and emotions); and to even protect your coming in and going out. Day and night, God is your guard. He never sleeps as He surrounds you with His protection.

In your travels, God will surround you. When you're doing business, He'll surround you. When you're being verbally attacked, He'll place a protective hedge around you, and the words of your accuser won't penetrate you.

Never forget: You may feel like you're being surrounded by the forces of your enemy, but the truth is that you're surrounded by Almighty God.

Surrounded by God's Army

You're actually in much the same position the old prophet Elisha was in when he and his assistant Gehazi were threatened by the Aramean army. You remember what happened in that situation. Gehazi was terrified and cried out, "Oh sir, what will we do now?"[19] But Elisha was perfectly calm.

God had been telling him for some time what the Aramean army had been plotting. He knew those soldiers were coming. So he responded to Gehazi with confidence and said:

"Don't be afraid!" Elisha told him. "For there are more on our side than on theirs!" Then Elisha prayed, "O Lord, open his eyes and let him see." The Lord opened the young man's eyes, and when he looked up, he saw the hillside around Elisha was filled with horses and chariots of fire. As the Aramean army advanced toward him, Elisha prayed, "O Lord, please make them blind." So the Lord struck them with blindness as Elisha had asked.[20]

Think of it! Elisha and Gehazi were surrounded by a powerful army of Heaven's warriors. God had sent them to protect and deliver His prophet from the enemies who'd planned to attack him. He did the same for Allen Shook in Albania as the country fell into civil war. Allen and his group may not have been able to see the angelic forces that surrounded them, but their safe escape indicates clearly those forces were there.

God is the same now as He was in Elisha and Gehazi's day. So, in perilous times when you feel surrounded and there seems to be no way out, lift your head, raise your hands in praise, and look to the Source of your deliverance. Put your faith in the promise God has made to you—He has you surrounded.

The Hiding Place

In Psalm 32:7, King David said to the Lord, "You are my hiding place; You shall preserve me from trouble; You shall surround me with songs of deliverance."[21] The word *songs* David used there refers to a *shout*. It tells us that God has already surrounded us with His shouts of deliverance.

Now it's your turn to put that shout in *your* mouth. To say in the face of every danger and demonic threat, "I have a covenant with Almighty God that promises to deliver me from the power of darkness and from every attack ever thrown at me!"

Because the hedge that *keeps* and *preserves* you is built with the words of God's promises, such shouts of deliverance strengthen your position. So, keep speaking and keep that hedge strong. Guard your thoughts and your mouth to make sure that *your* words agree with *God's* Word.

Then you can rest assured that you're safe and secure. The evil one can't lay a hand on you!

THE UNTOUCHABLES

O n September 11, 2001, Steve took his usual route to
work: the train from Pelham, New York, to Grand
Central Station in Midtown Manhattan. From there
he took the subway to Lower Manhattan. Hurrying up the
stairs from the subway, he heard people screaming. Looking
up, he watched in horror as an airplane flew into the North
Tower of the World Trade Center.

Nothing made sense. Certainly not the sound of an airplane engine in downtown Manhattan. Not the sight of the
crash or the fireball that exploded out of the building scatter-
ing debris over the smoke-filled streets like confetti. His mind
couldn't process the people who, driven by smoke and flames,
leapt from the building to their death.

*How had that pilot made such a mistake? What a horrible,
senseless accident*, Steve thought.

Knowing that his wife was busy teaching school, Steve phoned his parents. "Turn on the television!" he said. "Something is going on down here!"

As chief operations officer for Faith Exchange Church, Steve walked through screaming crowds, smoke and debris to get to his office. Located at 90 West Street, it was in Battery Park on the Hudson River. It was the closest building to the South Tower, the church met on the 18th floor.

Continuing his walk to work, Steve heard the voice of the Lord. *"Don't go any further."*

While the words didn't sound like a suggestion, Steve thought he must have misunderstood. The plane crash was an awful accident, but people needed to get to work. He'd walked another block when the Lord spoke another warning.

"DON'T GO ANY FURTHER!"

Steve froze in place. There was no mistaking that voice or that warning. Before he could turn around, he heard the drone of another engine. Looking up, he watched in disbelief as another airplane flew full-throttle into the South Tower.

Dear God, this isn't an accident! We're under attack!

"I was only a block away, on the side where a fireball mushroomed out of the building," Steve recalls. "Realizing that I would be hit by debris, I had a split second to decide whether to run across the Brooklyn Bridge on foot or take the subway. I decided on the subway. I ran down the stairs where a train sat waiting. I jumped on the train and the doors closed behind me. After I left town, the entire transit system was shut down. Most of the cell phones were out of service. At home, I shuddered as I watched the South Tower collapse into *our* church building! If God hadn't stopped me from going to work, I would have died.

"I thought of all the times Pastor Dan Stratton had taught on the protection available to those who prayed and confessed Psalm 91. I prayed that psalm almost every single day. I prayed it over my wife and kids. Over my parents and the church. I can't count how many times we had prayed that psalm over the 18th floor that housed our church. We'd prayed over our computers and every chair.

"We'd also pled the blood of Jesus over everything. We believed our covenant with God covered it all. Still, as the building burned, I wondered how anything could survive.

"I learned later that Pastor Dan had been uptown at a breakfast. He'd stood on a balcony and watched the events unfold. Jimmy, our CFO, was sitting at his desk talking on the phone when the plane hit the South Tower. Throwing down the phone, he'd run down the stairs, surviving the carnage. My wife had watched it from her classroom window. As time passed, we realized that the church structure was our only casualty. Every member had survived."

Ten days later, Steve climbed the stairs to the 18th floor to the church with a police escort. They were hoping to recover the computer hard drives if they hadn't melted in the fire. As they passed each floor from one to 17, Steve's heart dropped as he saw that each floor was nothing more than a burned-out shell. There was nothing left.

Chills rippled up his spine as they reached the 18th floor. Miraculously, it hadn't burned. Every chair, computer, book and Bible was intact. The only damage had been from smoke. Steve let the realization wash over him.

Not a soul from his church died. Not a single thing burned.

Turning to one of the policemen, Steve asked, "What about the floors above us, 19 through 23? Are they like ours? Smoke damage only?"

"No," the officer said shaking his head, a strange look on his face, "every floor in the building burned—except yours."

All these years later, Steve is still in awe of God's protection. What is his advice to those facing perilous times?

"Put your trust in Jesus," he says. "Pray Psalm 91. And never, ever forget that there is power in the blood of Jesus."

Steve will certainly never forget it. The worst terrorist attack in the history of the nation, and they were at ground zero. The entire building burned except for the 18th floor, home of Faith Exchange Church. Only those who made a habit of praying for God's protection escaped the carnage.

The Favor of God

It's often said that God doesn't show favoritism. That He loves everyone the same, so He wouldn't pass over one person to favor another. But that's not entirely accurate.

Although God *loves* all people equally, He does *favor* certain people. Although His blessings and benefits are meant to be enjoyed by every person, some people are left to deal with their problems on their own, while others find God's help and are visited by His supernatural provision and protection.

What makes the difference?

It's a matter of faith and obedience.

According to the Bible, God's eyes are constantly looking across the earth for someone—*anyone*—whose heart is loyal to Him so He can show Himself strong on their behalf. [22] He's always looking and longing for those who will connect with His blessing and power—those who will live by His Word and yield to His authority in their lives.

Satan, on the other hand, is always looking for those who aren't living that way. Those who due to lack of knowledge, unbelief, or rebellion have left themselves vulnerable to him. He doesn't care whether they're church-goers or unbelievers. He'll visit his destructive plans on anybody he can.

You've seen it happen many times: Even good people fall prey to terrible things that could have been avoided if they'd only been listening to God's voice and living under His promises of protection.

This reality is revealed in the Book of Exodus in one of the most dramatic events in all of history—the deliverance of the Israelites out of Egypt on the night of the first Passover. That event has been celebrated by the Jews for thousands of years. For them it's a reminder not only of how God liberated them from bondage but of how He protected them during a dark night of terror and death.

For the Egyptians though, that first Passover night was a different experience altogether: Heart-breaking. Dreadful. Multiplied thousands dead. Someone in every household died. Not a single Egyptian family remained untouched by grief.

What's worse, it didn't have to happen. They'd been warned by God in advance and told how to avoid it. God had sent Moses and Aaron to Pharaoh numerous times with the same message. "Let my people go."

Pharaoh, however, had refused. "I won't do it!" he said. "We like the slave labor. We can't continue to build without it."

God sent plague after plague to get Pharaoh's attention. He warned him time and again. Finally, Moses told Pharaoh that the first born of every living person and animal in Egypt would die if he didn't set the Israelites free from slavery. But even then, Pharaoh said, "No!"

That night was pierced with screams of heartbroken mothers and fathers. Even the Palace echoed with the sound of grief. After the death angel passed over Egypt, the son of Pharaoh himself lay dead.

Yet on that same night, millions of Israelites enjoyed total safety. The destruction passed over them, and they not only survived, "there was not one feeble person among their tribes."[23] What's the explanation? The Israelites marked the doorposts of their houses with the blood of a lamb, as God had instructed. They did what He said and were spared.

It was that simple.

While the world around them paid the price for their resistance to God, the Israelites were preserved by the price paid by the sacrificial lamb. The lamb's blood became the substitute for their own blood. As they applied that blood to the doorposts of their households, God separated them out as His own special people.

They embraced their identity as His nation and sealed their new consecration. Their outward separation from Egypt would be accompanied by an inward separation from everything Egyptian, or contrary to God.

Blood of the Lamb

The Passover lamb, of course, pointed forward in time to Jesus. Several thousand years later, His blood would be sprinkled on the heavenly mercy seat on behalf of all mankind. Just as the lamb's blood defeated death on Passover, the life in Jesus' blood defeated sin and death once and for all. His sacrifice demanded that the power of death, disease, and destruction pass over *you*.

That's really what the first Passover was all about! It was a picture of the deliverance Jesus has provided for every man, woman, and child throughout the course of human history.

His sacrifice applied to the doorposts of your heart will bring to you the power of the Passover. It will separate you from the world and deliver you into a new life of God's grace and fellowship. It will make available to you the same safety, good health, and ample provision the Israelites enjoyed the night God freed them from the slavery of Egypt.

There is protection from danger and death in the blood sacrifice of Jesus Christ!

That's why on the 18th floor of that building the Faith Exchange Church didn't burn. It *couldn't* burn because it was under God's supernatural protection. It had to be preserved, not because its members were super-spiritual and deserved to live while others deserved to die, but because they understood and applied the power of Jesus' blood.

They prayed and confessed Psalm 91 over themselves, their families and the property. They believed essentially the same thing the Israelites did during Passover: That because, in the spirit, the blood of the Lamb had been sprinkled over their doorposts, destruction would have to pass over them.

What about the good Christian people who do experience destruction in such situations? Shouldn't the blood of Jesus work the same way for them? Yes, and it will if they know how to apply it and act accordingly. But many Christians don't, so the words spoken in Hosea 4:6 come to pass in their lives: "My people are destroyed for lack of knowledge...." [24]

Notice God didn't say that His people perish for a lack of power. He didn't even say they perish for a lack of goodness. He said a lack of knowledge is the problem. They haven't been taught how to access the protection that's available to them in God.

Become Untouchable

Such protection is available though, to all of us. Hebrews 10:22 makes it clear. It tells us we can all "draw near [to God] with a true heart in full assurance of faith, having our hearts sprinkled from an evil conscience, and our bodies washed with pure water."[25] We can all have confidence that we've been delivered—spirit, soul, and body—from the grip of our enemy. We can all partake of the assurance of God's protective covering because Jesus' blood was sprinkled for our deliverance from sin.

Satan cannot cross the line of the blood sacrifice of Jesus.

That supernatural line puts an end to the works of darkness. When we accept Jesus' sacrifice and embrace His life, we walk out of bondage and step across that blood line into a new life in God. We take on a new identity as God's special and holy people and we're separated from the spirit and destruction of the world.

The Passover Lamb has become the mighty Lion of the tribe of Judah. He has risen to the highest place of power. He's set us free to stand with Him confident and secure, safe from the enemy's attacks, in supernatural peace and security.

When He's on your side, you don't have to fear what your enemies can do to you because from Satan's point of view, you've become untouchable. As First John 5:18 says in *The Message* Bible, "The God-begotten are also the God-protected. The Evil One can't lay a hand on them."

Let this sink in!

You are untouchable and God-protected. Satan can't lay a hand on you. He has no right to touch you, your family, your health, your money, or your property when the blood is on the doorposts of your heart. The Lamb of God has brought you under His umbrella of His protection, cleansed you, and given you the strength to overcome any strategy of the enemy. You are in the secret place of the Most High, covered with His love and light.

Just as the children of Israel walked out of Egypt, you can walk *out of* any bondage and *into* a life full of supernatural protection and provision. So, believe it and do it. Take your stand in that place of supernatural protection by faith in the sacrificial blood of Jesus. Become one of God's *untouchables*.

POWERFUL PROMISES
OF PROTECTION

All the Bible's heroes of faith, whose exploits leap off the pages sparking faith in us so many centuries later, share a common thread: faith in God. They each embraced God's Word and His promises with uncommon confidence.

Moses. Daniel. Shadrach, Meshach and Abednego. David. Paul. Peter. John. Stephen...

Jesus.

Their courage proved to be larger than life, we can be sure, because God's promises traveled from their minds to their hearts. Nourished by those promises, their faith grew and became great. So great, that regardless of the dangers they faced, they trusted God to keep them.

Both Old and New Testaments are filled with scriptural promises of protection. But nowhere do we find promises more powerful than those in Psalm 91. It contains God's definitive word on the matter. Countless stories from World Wars I and II, Vietnam, Desert Storm, Israel, Afghanistan, and Iraq detail accounts of troops who quoted Psalm 91 every day and lost not a single soldier in their company, despite incredible odds.

Today, each of us have as much right to pray these promises and receive them by faith as those on the front lines.

Psalm 91:

He who dwells in the secret place of the Most High
Shall abide under the shadow of the Almighty.
I will say of the LORD, "He is my refuge and my fortress;
My God, in Him I will trust."
Surely He shall deliver you from the snare of the fowler
And from the perilous pestilence.
He shall cover you with His feathers,
And under His wings you shall take refuge;
His truth shall be your shield and buckler.
You shall not be afraid of the terror by night,
Nor of the arrow that flies by day,
Nor of the pestilence that walks in darkness,
Nor of the destruction that lays waste at noonday.
A thousand may fall at your side,
And ten thousand at your right hand;
But it shall not come near you.

Only with your eyes shall you look,
And see the reward of the wicked.
Because you have made the LORD, who is my refuge,
Even the Most High, your dwelling place,
No evil shall befall you,
Nor shall any plague come near your dwelling;
For He shall give His angels charge over you,
To keep you in all your ways.
In their hands they shall bear you up,
Lest you dash your foot against a stone.
You shall tread upon the lion and the cobra,
The young lion and the serpent you shall trample underfoot.
Because he has set his love upon Me,
therefore I will deliver him; I will set him on high,
because he has known My name.
He shall call upon Me, and I will answer him;
I will be with him in trouble;
I will deliver him and honor him.
With long life I will satisfy him,
And show him My salvation.[26]

How to Receive

Every aspect of this amazing psalm reveals God's Covenant protection for every believer. So why doesn't everyone walk in this supernatural protection? For the same reason not everyone will be born again even though Jesus has paid the price for the sins of all mankind. God's promises are conditional. They must be believed and received. We're given the condition to the promise of salvation in Romans 10:9-10:

> If you confess with your mouth the Lord Jesus and believe in your heart that God has raised Him from the dead, you will be saved. For with the heart one believes unto righteousness, and with the mouth confession is made unto salvation. [27]

To enjoy the salvation Jesus provided for us on Calvary, we must first believe it in our hearts and then speak it with our mouths. The same is true when it comes to God's protection. To fully enjoy it, we must first believe and speak what the Bible says about it. We must look to God and trust the magnificent promises He's given us in passages like Psalm 91.

What a wonderful picture of protection that psalm presents!

It reveals God as our refuge, our fortress, and our covering. It depicts His Word as a shield that protects us from the arrows and missiles of our enemy. It shows His angels standing ready to go to work on our behalf to keep us safe.

Growing up in God includes growing in His provision of protection. He tells us in this psalm of the many ways He desires to keep us under the shadow of His protection. But He expects us to grow in our faith and increase in our ability to trust Him to deliver us.

Three separate times Psalm 91 declares that God will deliver us! Each time it describes the deliverance coming in a different way. There is a progression in the words the psalmist uses that parallels the growth in our Christian lives. He may not deliver us the way we expect Him to, but He will always be faithful to us. He'll never leave us on our own.

Snatch Out of Trouble

The first time in Psalm 91 God tells us that He will deliver us is found in verse 3: "Surely He shall deliver you from the snare of the fowler and from the perilous pestilence."

The word *deliver* in this instance means *to pluck up or snatch up out of trouble*. It speaks of the kind of rescue that's needed when someone gets caught in a trap. Think about a wild animal, for instance. In the wild, it roams around freely, at will. It spends its day looking for food and staying away from predators. But it can be caught unaware by a snare that's been laid by a skilled hunter. It can wind up in trouble because it didn't see the trap until it's too late.

Had the animal been watching, it might have seen and avoided the danger. But once ensnared, it's helpless. It can't get away. All it can do is wait for the trapper to come and finish the job.

As Christians, we sometimes find ourselves in the same kind of fix. We're ensnared by our enemy who lays out his traps and then waits for us to walk into them and become helpless in his grip. So often when this happens, we could have been more aware of the potential problems that awaited us. But for whatever reason, we weren't. So we got caught.

There's good news for us, however. God is still on our side. He doesn't leave us to struggle through on our own. We still have a Deliverer! He will take hold of us when we put our faith in His Word and snatch us right out of the snare that has entrapped us.

Psalm 124:7-8 says, "Our soul has escaped as a bird from the snare of the fowlers; The snare is broken, and we have escaped. Our help is in the name of the Lord, Who made heaven and earth."[28]

Just as the bird caught in the snare must have help in order to escape, we too need help from Heaven to set us free from Satan's grasp—and that help is ever available to us. It is found in the matchless Name of Jesus. So call on Him when you find yourself facing desperate times. He'll answer you! He'll pluck you up out of trouble and put you under the shadow of His wings where His peace reigns.

Carry to Safety

The second mention of God's deliverance in Psalm 91 is found in verse 14: "Because he has set his love upon Me, therefore I will deliver him; I will set him on high, because he has known My name."

In this instance, the Hebrew word translated *deliver* is different from the one in verse 3. This word means *to lift and carry to safety*. Rather than referring to a rescue that takes place after you're already caught in a snare, it speaks of a deliverance that takes place beforehand; of God coming to your aid in advance.

When God lifts you up before difficult times come and carries you through them, you can avoid the snares Satan sets in your path. You can stay safe in the calm harbor God has created for you even while around you the storms of life rage.

Proverbs 13:14 says, "The teaching of the wise is a fountain of life, that one may avoid the snares of death."[29] The more we meditate on the teaching of God's Word and His ways, the more wise we grow in our ability to avoid the snares set for us.

Paul experienced this kind of deliverance when he was traveling on a ship to Rome to stand before Caesar. During the trip, the ship was caught in a terrible storm. It was destroyed in the raging sea, and Paul was marooned on the island of Malta.

Before those things happened though, God warned Paul about them. God alerted him that there was trouble ahead, and Paul passed the warning along to those in charge of the ship. If they had listened, they could have avoided the storm completely. But they didn't. They chose to listen to the captain instead of Paul. They stuck with their original plan and sailed right into disaster.

Their decision ultimately cost them their ship and all their cargo, but before the tragedy claimed their lives, Paul heard from God again. In the belly of that prison ship, chained to the hull, he had a visitation from an angel. The angel came with a message of hope and a promise of protection which Paul shared with all those on board.

> And now I urge you to take heart, for there will be no loss of life among you, but only of the ship. For there stood by me this night an angel of the God to whom I belong and whom I serve, saying, 'Do not be afraid, Paul; you must be brought before Caesar; and indeed God has granted you all those who sail with you.' Therefore take heart, men, for I believe God that it will be just as it was told me. However, we must run aground on a certain island.[30]

This is a clear description of God giving aid in advance. It shows how He can provide safety and calm even during life-threatening trouble.

That storm came to take Paul's life because he was such a threat to the kingdom of darkness. But it couldn't get the job done. Paul made it through unharmed because he was listening to and obeying God, calling on Him rather than focusing on the perils of the sea. God had given Paul an assignment to preach the Gospel in Rome to Caesar and no storm hell could whip up would stop them!

Because Paul connected by faith to God's delivering power, not only did he complete his trip, but none of his fellow travelers lost their lives.

Equipped for Battle

The last instance of the word *deliver* in Psalm 91 is found in verses 15-16.

> He shall call upon Me, and I will answer him; I will be with him in trouble; I will deliver him and honor him. With long life I will satisfy him, and show him My salvation.[31]

This final statement contains yet a third Hebrew word. It means *to deliver by equipping for battle*. This word is used because in these verses, although God promises to be with us in trouble, He does *not* promise trouble won't find us. Although He says our deliverance will come, He does not say we'll be delivered by avoiding all trouble.

Instead, in this instance God indicates we'll be delivered by the spiritual equipment He has given us to stand up to adversity without being swayed or stopped. We'll be delivered as we use the spiritual weapons God has given us to enforce the devil's defeat.

You do have such weapons, you know!

As Second Corinthians 10:4 says, these weapons are "not carnal but mighty in God for pulling down strongholds." [32]

They're not weapons of flesh and blood, but weapons of spiritual warfare identified in Ephesians 6:17 as "the sword of the Spirit, which is the word of God."[33]

His Word in our mouth becomes the equipment and weapon of war to blast through the enemy's strategies. Notice Second Timothy 3:16 from the Phillips translation:

> All scripture is inspired by God and is useful for teaching the faith and correcting error, for resetting the direction of a man's life and training him in good living. The scriptures are the comprehensive equipment of the man of God, and fit him fully for all branches of his work.

God's Word is the equipment that we use in the face of every attack. The power to deliver us comes through our own words of dominion. But it's the mature believer who practices the habit of speaking according to God's Word and not the circumstances.

When you put God's Word in your mouth and your prayers, you release His power to go to work for you. So use the Word like the sword it is. Wield it with skill and impose God's will and His Word on the circumstances that confront you. Turn your own words into mighty spiritual tools and weapons of battle. Launch an attack that darkness will not be able to withstand.

When Satan comes against you, conquer him by declaring powerful promises of God like this one in Isaiah:

No weapon that is formed against you shall prosper, and every tongue that shall rise against you in judgment you shall show to be in the wrong. This [peace, righteousness, security, triumph over opposition] is the heritage of the servants of the Lord [those in whom the ideal Servant of the Lord is reproduced]; this is the righteousness or the vindication which they obtain from Me [this is that which I impart to them as their justification], says the Lord.[34]

This is the mature believer's mindset. Our thoughts won't fall into despair and fear over the battle that may be raging. We will avoid the snares of our enemy. We not only avoid trouble, but we will take a firm grip on the weapons of war God has provided us and wield His power effectively with the assurance that His Word is all powerful.

So fill your words with faith in God's Word. Declare that He is your Deliverer and that *no* hellish strategy formed against you can succeed. You have God's angels surrounding you with all His resources available to you. His words in Isaiah 41:10 are His words to *you*, no matter what you may face in this life: "Fear not, for I am with you; Be not dismayed, for I am your God. I will strengthen you, Yes, I will help you, I will uphold you with My righteous right hand." [35]

THE GUARDIAN
OF YOUR HEART

Afghanistan, David Stowe, Jr.

On Friday March 13, 2009, William David Stowe, Jr. climbed into a Ground Utility Vehicle with his Team Commander and other members of his unit. Stationed near Delaram in Nimruz Province of Afghanistan, David was part of a three-day operation designed to stabilize villages by creating relationships with the people. The goal was to encourage them to work with the United States military to remove the Taliban from the area.

There'd been multiple reports of suicide bombers driving motorcycles and other vehicles in the area. Along the route, the US convoy stopped at numerous checkpoints with the Afghanistan National Police and the Afghanistan National Army. Most days, David rode in the back of what resembled

69

a small pickup bed. Today, however, he sat in the cab behind the driver. Passing through the rough, rocky desert terrain, he kept a careful watch of their surroundings.

Texas, Vikki Burke

I sat reading my Bible on my front porch at home in Texas when I sensed a great urgency to pray for Davey Stowe's protection. I'd met his parents when they moved to Texas to attend a local Bible institute where I taught. After graduating, they'd moved back to North Carolina where they started a church. When Davey had been deployed to Afghanistan, they'd asked several of their friends to pray for him.

When I sensed the urgency to pray, I knew Davey was in severe trouble. Although I had no idea what was going on, I knew it was serious. Life or death serious.

I prayed protection from the scriptures over him and took authority over the plot of the enemy to kill him. When I sensed the danger had passed, I sent a text to his parents.

"I don't know what's going on with Davey, but I have been seriously praying for his protection."

North Carolina, David's Parents

The night before, during the Stowe's church service, things hadn't gone as planned. The meeting had begun as usual with praise and worship, but when David Stowe, Sr. had tried to move on to the next part of the service and get into his message, it felt like he ran into a brick wall.

He began praying in the Spirit.

When he tried to preach again, he hit that wall.

Each time that happened, he prayed. Before he'd realized it, they'd spent the entire service praying in the Spirit. By the time they'd sensed a release, the service had been over.

The next morning, they got my text message telling them I'd sensed an urgency to pray for Davey's protection. *Had that been why the Lord had them pray in the Spirit all evening?* they wondered.

Afghanistan, David Stowe, Jr.

Davey had just rolled up his ballistic-glass window when a light blue pickup approached their convoy. The lead vehicle waved the driver away. When he didn't move away, they fired warning shots to get him to pull over.

The driver pulled the pickup to the side of the road. As the convoy passed, he pulled out in front of Davey's vehicle. The turret gunman fired more warning shots. He swerved off the road once again, only to move parallel with Davey's vehicle.

Davey looked at the driver with a note of alarm.

He was clean shaven.

Suicide bombers often shave just before they die.

The pickup truck exploded next to Davey's door. The driver's clean-shaven face was the last thing Davey saw.

Death Comes Calling

When Davey regained consciousness, his vehicle was on fire. The tires were all flat. Everyone inside was alive but just regaining consciousness. The blast had blown Davey's unarmored door open and his rifle out of the vehicle.

They found nothing left of the blue pickup except an axle. They put the fire out in their vehicle and towed it back to headquarters. The blast residue was tested and determined to be a very powerful explosive. Experts couldn't explain why Davey's vehicle hadn't been obliterated. Nor did they know how the men inside had survived, but Davey knew.

Through intelligence, it was later revealed that the Afghanistan National Police had relayed the team's exact location to the Taliban. The Team Commander had been the Taliban's target.

Davey knew God's hand had protected them that day. He'd been taught to believe for such protection all his life. "From an early age, we'd imparted the powerful promises in Psalm 91 to him," says his mother, Wendy. "In addition to our praying for him, he was taught to speak the Word of God and to plead the blood of Jesus over himself and his team—which he did daily.

"After the suicide bombing, we calculated the time difference and realized that Vikki had been praying at the same time it was happening. She was in Texas. We were in North Carolina. And our son was in Afghanistan. God used all our prayers to get them out alive."

Say What God Says

Davey has a destiny in God. When the Taliban dared threatened it, God intervened.

Like Davey, you as a believer have a destiny too. And when it's threatened God will also intervene for you.

God doesn't do miracles for those who whine and cry in order to get Him to help them. Although He has mercy on those who do that, it shouldn't be our M.O. as New Testament believers. No, Jesus taught in Mark 11:23 that we're to deal with contrary situations by speaking words of faith. He said, as Job 22:28 does, "…Declare a thing, and it will be established for you."[36]

That doesn't mean whatever we spout from our mouths will just happen. It means when we speak "God's Word in faith,"[37] it will come to pass. This is spiritual law: If we want to attain the hope and a future God has planned for us, we must declare what He says. And, like Davey, we must do so even in the face of contrary evidence.

That's not always easy. It goes against the ways of the world. The world is always flowing in a pessimistic and destructive direction. So, speaking words of faith requires you to swim against the current. While that can be difficult sometimes, you can do it because Jesus made a powerful statement about His first disciples. He said about them: "They are no more defined by the world than I am defined by the world."[38] If you are His disciple, then you have the same advantage as the first disciples.

You don't have to talk like the world does because your identity as a born-again child of God is not of this world. You're not defined by it any more than Jesus is. You can reject its pessimistic predictions, start declaring God's Word and tap into a new and powerful way of living.

Of course, the world won't like it when you do that. It always reacts with hostility when believers refuse to participate in its way of doing things. When Jesus gave His disciples God's Word, He said, "the godless world hated them because of it."[39] The world will react the same way toward you. But that's okay. Forget about what the world thinks. Stay with the Word and enjoy a blessed lifestyle!

In the World but Not of It

It *is* God's will for you to be blessed while you're still on the earth, you know. He didn't intend for you to wait until you get to Heaven to enjoy His blessings. He planned for you to enjoy a heavenly life here on earth.

When Jesus prayed for us in John 17:15, He said to the Father, "I'm not asking you to take them out of the world, but to keep them safe from the evil one." In other words, He prayed that while we're living in the world, it would not live in us. Although we may be attacked with some of the same difficulties the world is, we won't experience the same outcome.

Jesus never said God was going to remove all trouble from our lives. He said, "Here on earth you will have many trials and sorrows. But take heart, because I have overcome the world."[40]

Often when I talk about how we can live victoriously in this world and be protected from the evil one, people bring up the story of Job from the Old Testament. "What about him?" they ask. "Doesn't the Bible say that even though he was a righteous man, God removed the hedge of protection around him and let the devil get to him?"

No, that's not what the Bible says at all. Religious tradition has taught that over the years, but it's not true. God wasn't the one who allowed bad things to happen to Job. He wasn't Job's hedge-remover. He was Job's hedge-provider, just as He is ours.

A hedge is defined as *a fence, wall, barrier,* or *limit.* It's the protective barrier God puts around His people to insulate us from Satan's plans and attacks. It's designed to make us invincible to the attacks of the kingdom of darkness, and in Job's life, that's exactly what it did.

According to Scripture, Satan wanted to break down the wall of protection around Job but he couldn't. All he could do was complain about it and accuse God of being unfair. Admitting he was powerless to harm Job, Satan said to God, "You have always put a wall of protection around him and his home and his property…Why, no one ever had it so good! You pamper him like a pet, make sure nothing bad ever happens to him or his family or his possessions, bless everything he does—he can't lose!"[41]

Actually, what Satan said was, "God, You're too good to Your people. I can't ruin and wreak havoc in their lives because of Your protection." As if that was an indictment!

Pulling Down the Hedge

That's not all Satan said, either. Once he'd registered his complaint, he went on to essentially dare God to remove Job's hedge of protection. "What do you think would happen," he said, "if you reached down and took away everything that is his?"[42]

God didn't take the devil's dare, of course. There's no way He could remove the protection He'd set in place around Job. Protection is, after all, a *covenant promise* of God and He is a promise keeper. He cannot, and will not, break the covenant He's made with His people. So, Satan was left on his own to pursue the only option available to him.

He would have to deceive and manipulate Job into destroying the wall of protection himself.

Sure enough, that's what happened. Job fell for Satan's trick and pulled down his own hedge.

How did he do it?

That's an important question. If we are to prevent the hedge of protection from being penetrated in our own lives, we need to know the answer to it. And Job himself gave it to us. He said, "What I always feared has happened to me. What I dreaded has come true."[43]

Job wasn't indicating that he'd had just a fleeting thought about disaster. He was revealing a habit of worry that dominated his thinking. He'd worried about the *what if's* to the point where he wasn't just a little alarmed—the King James translation says Job *greatly* feared.

Great fear isn't the result of one thought, one word, or a few negative news broadcasts. Great fear is the result of hearing and hearing on an ongoing basis what the *world* says. Fear is a magnet that attracts disaster and ruin into our lives, just as it did for Job. It distracts us from the Word of God, causes us to meditate on the lies of the devil, and pulls our hedge down.

Job Dreaded

Fear is to the kingdom of darkness what faith is to the Kingdom of God. In the same way faith opens the door to

God, fear opens the door to the devil. Faith is the substance of things hoped for, but fear is the substance of things dreaded. It gives Satan the opportunity to bring into your life the things you worry and stress over.

Job was afraid of losing everything—his house, his family, his wealth, and his health. And fear produced those losses. It brought those things to pass in his life. When Job yielded to fear, he experienced the destruction common to the world because he'd compromised God's hedge of protection.

Ecclesiastes 10:8 says, "…Whoso breaketh an hedge, a serpent shall bite him."[44] Isaiah says if the hedge is removed and the wall broken down, that which has been protected shall be trodden down.[45] Job proved those things to be true. But we as born-again believers don't have to make the same mistake.

We can prove out instead what Jesus said about us—that we're no more defined by the world than *He* was defined by the world. We don't have to worry about the future when we hear negative reports about the economy, healthcare, or any other evil thing the world declares. We can say out loud: "That may be how the world is defined, but that's not how my household will live. The Bible says the righteous are encompassed with a shield, and I won't remove my hedge of protection by yielding to fear."

Fear of the Devil

"Yes," somebody might say, "but all this talk about the devil still scares me. I hate to admit it but I'm afraid of him."

I understand. I used to be fear based too, but then I found out what the Bible said about the authority God has given to believers. If you've never studied the subject, I urge you to do so.

It's a game changer.

Your fear of the devil will dissipate, just as mine did, when you realize that Jesus has given you His authority:

"Look, I have given you authority over all the power of the enemy, and you can walk among snakes and scorpions and crush them. Nothing will injure you."[46]

You'll stop being scared when you realize that our Heavenly Father "has *delivered us from the power of darkness* and conveyed *us* into the kingdom of the Son of His love."[47]

The New Testament makes it clear: you don't have to let the devil intimidate you. Through Jesus' death, burial and resurrection He disarmed the devil and took him captive. He took all the devil's authority away from him. Now all authority in heaven and on earth belongs to Jesus and He's given that authority to everyone who believes on Him.[48]

That's why in Mark 16:17 Jesus said that those of us who believe on Him will cast out demons. We can cast them out because we have authority over them! They must obey when we speak to them in Jesus' name, because, "At the name of Jesus every knee should bow, in heaven and on earth and under the earth."[49]

The enemy is a defeated foe! All you must do is enforce his defeat by exercising your authority over Him in the Name of Jesus and speak God's Word.

If you do those two things, and you find that fear continues to be a problem in your life, consider turning off the news. Stop listening to all the fear-peddling voices that clamor for your attention. Spend extra time focusing on what God promised you. The Word will anchor your mind and emotions and keep your hedge of supernatural protection intact.

Your Hedge of Protection

You may not be able to see that hedge of protection with your natural eyes, but you can see it with the eyes of your faith. Like Davey, you can believe what God's Word says about it and enjoy the safety and protection it provides.

If you live in worry though and keep listening to the voices of doom and gloom, you'll get the same results the world does. You'll wind up operating according to its wisdom, which is "earthly, sensual, and demonic."[50] The world's wisdom contradicts God's wisdom. It will distract you from God's promises. It will replace your faith with fear, tear down your hedge, and leave you vulnerable to the devil.

Proverbs 4:23 instructs us to: "Guard your heart above all else, for it determines the course of your life." That doesn't just mean guard your heart from what's wicked and perverse. It means guard it against anything that isn't in agreement with God's Word and His will.

Just as Adam was responsible for the Garden of Eden, you're responsible for the garden of your heart. It's your responsibility—not God's—to guard and tend it. So, determine right now to do whatever it takes to keep your hedge of protection up. If you've yielded to worry and fear, start building the hedge back up again. Spend time meditating on what God says so that your life will begin to reflect His blessings, and like Davey Stowe, you'll be protected no matter what comes your way.

HOLDING BACK DISASTER

I sat in my rocking chair on the front porch and basked in the simple pleasure of being home. Ours was an international ministry which required a lot of travel. Although I never tired of ministry opportunities, after decades of travel, I'd grown weary of the traveling part of it. When Dennis mentioned that he wanted us to take a road trip on our motorcycle, I was excited. That kind of travel was less tiring than long flights. Then he described the route.

New Zealand.

He wanted to ride his motorcycle from the north island of New Zealand to the south. I couldn't imagine a more beautiful journey or a more intimate way to visit one of the most beautiful countries on earth. I would enjoy every moment of the journey—except the flight.

To fly from DFW to Christchurch was 21 hours and 30 minutes. The flight to Queenstown was 22 hours. The shortest, to Auckland, was 18 hours and 20 minutes. One way.

I wished the Lord could just beam me there. The thought of another international flight was exhausting. I needed some down time. Rocking on my front porch was just the speed I needed.

Although Dennis had been disappointed, he understood. He'd headed out by himself to ride across New Zealand. Following that trip, he was scheduled to preach in Maui, and I'd agreed to meet him there.

Every time I envisioned Dennis on the other side of the world having the time of his life, I felt impressed to pray Psalm 18:48. "You hold me safe beyond the reach of my enemies; you save me from violent opponents." I prayed that scripture and asked the Lord to keep Dennis in the secret place of the Most High—untouchable.

Over the two weeks Dennis was gone, I continued praying that verse. As I did, I thought a great deal about the place it describes—the place beyond the reach of our enemies. Which is, of course, the secret place of the Most High referred to in Psalm 91. Because the Lord had quickened the verse to me just after Dennis left for New Zealand, I assumed it was for his protection while he was there. But God had another reason for planting that scripture in my heart.

He knew what was to come.

84

The night before I was scheduled to fly to Maui and meet Dennis, I was awakened out of a deep sleep. As my eyes opened, I heard these words: *"What would you do if a tsunami hit Hawaii?"* Undisturbed, I answered, "I would move to higher ground. But You hold me safe beyond the reach of my enemies. You save me from violent opponents."

Then, without giving the question or the tsunami another thought, I went peacefully back to sleep. The next morning, I didn't even remember what had happened. I got up without any sense of concern, flew out early, and met Dennis in Maui on Friday afternoon. We settled into the hotel and planned to rest all day Saturday before Dennis began meetings Sunday morning.

But at 5:00 a.m. Saturday morning the phone began ringing. Dennis answered the phone although he was still quite drowsy after his flight from New Zealand. The pastor of the church Dennis was scheduled to speak for said, "An earthquake, registering 8.8 on the Richter scale, struck off the coast of Chile," he said. "There is now a tsunami bearing down on the Hawaiian Islands. They expect it to hit Maui at 11 a.m. People are in a panic trying to get off the island. There is only one road leading to your hotel, and it's blocked by traffic. I can't get to you, and you can't get out."

When Dennis relayed their conversation to me, I remembered being awakened the night before and told him about my experience. I told him how I'd been praying Psalm 18:48 for the past two weeks. At that moment, I realized my prayer had been regarding protection from the tsunami. We had supernatural peace because the Holy Spirit had already warned me of what was to come. He'd given me the scripture to stand on two weeks before the earthquake struck Chile.

We prayed together in agreement. "Father, You said in Matthew 18:19, 'If two of you agree here on earth concerning anything you ask, my Father in heaven will do it for you.' We ask for Your Word to act as a wall in the ocean. We forbid the tsunami from hitting any of the Pacific islands. We declare that it will hit our words in the ocean and bounce back. We pray this in Jesus' name."

Having settled that, we went down to breakfast and found the place in pandemonium as people checked out of the hotel, desperate to get a flight off the island. Our waitress was frantic about her children. "They're home alone!" she wailed. "I can't get to them, and they can't get to me!" We prayed for the safety of her children and she received the peace of God.

After breakfast, we decided to return to our room and take a nap because no one was allowed on the beach. When we woke, we checked the news to see what had happened.

Nothing.

The tsunami didn't hit Maui or any of the islands. The next day, the news reported that something odd had happened in the ocean. It was as though the tsunami had hit an invisible blockade and bounced back to Chile.

God's Creative Power

I know what you might be thinking. *She's nuts to think anyone could have control over a tsunami. People don't have that kind of power.*

Yes, they do. Especially when God's Word comes out of the mouths of Christians who know how to use the authority Jesus gave them. We have Christ—the Anointed One—Himself living in our hearts. The Christ who spoke to the wind and waves and they obeyed. The Christ who multiplied the loaves and fishes. The Christ who walked on water and raised people from the dead. The same Christ who said, "I tell you the truth, anyone who believes in me will do the same works I have done, and even greater works, because I am going to be with the Father."[51]

One of the keys to doing the works of Jesus is learning to speak as He did. Using our words to release His power into our lives and situations. It's declaring as Psalm 91:2 does, "This I declare about the Lord: He alone is my refuge, my place of safety; he is my God, and I trust him."

It's not just *thinking* God is our Refuge, our Fortress, and our Protector. It's not just *knowing* that He guides and keeps us as we follow His lead. It's *saying* those things—in our prayers, our declarations of faith, and our daily conversation. It's fixing our eyes on Him as our place to run for refuge *and speaking accordingly* that puts us in the place where we're protected from threats and attacks of every kind.

Why is what we say so important? Because from the very beginning, God created everything with His spoken words. You can see it all through the first chapter of Genesis. Time and again, on each of the first six days of creation, "God said, let there be...and there was...."

In Psalm 91:2 we find the same principle in operation. Only now, we're the ones doing the talking. We're abiding under the shelter of His protection as a result of what we say.

Our spoken words have power when we speak what God's Word says from a heart of faith. They bring us into agreement with the promises God has given to us and put us in the strongest possible position of faith—*and faith moves God.*

You can actually precede every scriptural promise God has given you with the words "I will say of the Lord." You can find out in the Word who God says He is and declare He is that to you. You can declare with confidence: "I will say of the Lord that He is my Protector. He is my Provider. He is my Healer. He delivers me from the hand of my enemies. He is my righteousness, my shield, my joy."

In fact, Jesus is to us *only* who *we* say He is. He is our Savior only when we declare He is. He is our Healer only when we say He is. He is our Baptizer in the Holy Spirit only when we say He is. *We* are the ones who establish how much of Jesus' influence He can bring into our lives.

If you're not receiving God's blessing on the level you desire, stop and ask yourself today: Who is Jesus to me, and what am I saying of the Lord? Am I consistent in what I say? Am I letting the problems I encounter in life dictate what I believe about God's promises? Or am I dictating to those problems the promises God has given me in His Word?

Listen to the Holy Spirit

"But Vikki," you might say, "there are thousands of promises in the Bible. How do I know which one I should be declaring in my current situation?"

You'll know by the leading of the Holy Spirit. Your relationship with Him gives you a wonderful advantage! He'll warn you before events happen, so you can either pray to influence those events or avoid them altogether. As John 16:13 says of the Holy Spirit, "He will guide you into all truth...He will tell you about the future."

He does this for all of us as believers all the time, but sometimes we miss what He's saying because we aren't paying attention. We become too busy with other things. Life's distractions fill our minds with what I call *static*, and we're hindered from hearing the Holy Spirit's voice.

It's like what happens when we're listening to a radio station while driving. If we travel too far from the source transmitting the broadcast, static will interfere with what we were listening to. And if we keep driving away from the source, before long we won't hear anything *but* static. All we must do to solve the problem, however, is get closer to the source. Then the signal will get stronger and we'll be able to hear the broadcast again.

In much the same way, the static from the world can interfere with our ability to hear the Holy Spirit. But the solution is simple. All we must do is draw closer to the Source of truth. Then we'll be able to hear what He is saying loud and clear.

You Will Hold Back Disasters

The reason the Holy Spirit warns us of an upcoming or potential disaster is so that we can pray and use our God-given authority to control the situation. "Believe me," He said in Matthew 18:18, "Whatever you forbid upon earth will be what is forbidden in Heaven, and whatever you permit on earth will be what is permitted in Heaven."[52] This verse clearly reveals that we have control over what we allow in our lives.

In Genesis 1:28, God gave us the assignment to have dominion and subdue the earth. What we do with it is our choice. We can either do nothing and by our lack of action permit the devil to have his way—or we can forbid disaster and change what the devil has planned.

Recently, when the weatherman announced a Category 5 hurricane was barreling down on the east coast, our friends began to use their God-given authority and forbid the hurricane from wreaking its havoc. Overnight the hurricane dropped to a Category 1 and veered away from the coastline.

When they exercised their God-given authority, disaster was avoided.

If we'll do the same, we won't be fearful when the Holy Spirit warns us of adverse things to come. Instead, we'll exercise the authority God has given us. Through *His* power, we'll change circumstances and live as overcomers during every situation.

A well-known and trusted prophet delivered this prophetic word in 1998 under the inspiration of the Holy Spirit:

"You will begin to hold back disasters that the devil had planned, not only in weather, not only in money, but also in politics and in the affairs of nations, for God Almighty is Ruler in the affairs of men. And when My Word is strong in your spirit and strong in your mouth, I will use you as a control point. And when disasters are planned, you will stand up and say, 'No!'"

In these perilous days, we should take those words to heart. We should believe them and say to God as Jeremiah 32:17 does, "Ah, Lord GOD! Behold, You have made the heavens and the earth by Your great power and outstretched arm. There is nothing too hard for You."[53]

Who could dispute God's ability to use us to help guard and keep safe what He created? Obviously, if He can make the heavens and the earth, He can handle anything that happens here. He is still saying as He did in verse 27 of that same chapter: "Behold, I am the Lord, the God of all flesh. Is there anything too hard for Me?"[54]

Nothing has ever been too hard for God when it comes to protecting His people!

By His great power, God used Moses to part the Red Sea. He brought all of Israel out of Egypt. He delivered Shadrach, Meshach and Abednego from the fiery furnace. He kept Daniel alive in the lion's den. He caused the walls around Jericho to fall. And He did all those things under the Old Covenant.

Hebrews 8:6 says, "Now Jesus, our High Priest, has been given a ministry that is far superior to the old priesthood, for he is the one who mediates for us a far better covenant with God, based on better promises." As believers we can say with confidence the words of the Apostle Paul. "For I know whom I have believed and I am convinced that He is able to guard what I have entrusted to Him until that day."

There has never been a more appropriate time to exercise our authority than the time we're living in right now. We are the Body of Christ. Let's allow Him to minister His Word through us to hold back disasters.

STAYING IN THE SHADE OF GOD'S PROTECTION

Dennis' flight to Paris had departed Dallas on time but was behind schedule arriving. The pilot announced the problem. "A volcano erupted in Iceland," he said. "Because of smoke and ash in the air, we've been diverted around it." As the plane landed in Paris, ash from the volcano was so bad that most of the planes in Europe, and an estimated 30,000 people were grounded.

It was 2010 and Dennis had been asked to speak in Paris. A few days later, he had a flight to Moscow, Russia where he'd been asked to minister with Rick and Denise Renner for a week.

Just after Dennis landed in Paris, that airport was closed. Airport officials had no idea when it would reopen. He landed on Saturday and preached the morning and evening services on Sunday. When he called the airport on Monday, it was still closed. People were in a panic to get home. A friend of ours took a train to Spain and flew back to the states from there. But by Monday every train out of Paris was sold out, as were all the cabins onboard ships.

The news coverage of the situation was stunning:

"The volcanic ash plume has disrupted most air travel in Northern Europe. Satellite images indicate that the volcano is emitting about 10,000 tons of carbon monoxide each day."

Dennis called the airport every few hours. It was still closed, and it didn't look as though it would be open in time for his flight to Russia on Wednesday.

Back home sitting on my front porch, I had been praying in the Spirit about the situation. Then I heard myself pray in English, "Wind," I declared, "you begin to blow from the east and from the south. Blow the ash out of the atmosphere and back to where it came."

All that day I thought about the prayer I'd prayed. The words sounded so familiar to me. I went to my Bible and started searching. Sure enough, I found Psalm 78:26, which says, "He caused an east wind to blow in the heavens; And by His power He brought the south wind."[55]

I've read the Bible from cover to cover, but I didn't consciously recall that particular verse. But the day I prayed for Dennis, the Holy Spirit brought it to my remembrance. That's why it's so important to build the Word in your heart and pray in the Spirit.

I texted Dennis and told him how the Holy Spirit had directed my prayer and encouraged him not to worry. I was confident he'd get to Russia as scheduled. But he was on the ground in Paris hearing all the bad reports—panic was in the atmosphere. He kept checking alternate transportation to Russia. Nothing.

By faith, Wednesday morning Dennis packed his bags and arrived at the airport even though it still hadn't reopened. He hung around the airport just waiting and waiting and waiting. Finally, he spoke to an agent at the gate but there was no new information. A few minutes later, miraculously his flight was announced. It was the first flight to leave Paris after the volcano had erupted.

He flew to Moscow just like he'd originally scheduled without a problem and fulfilled his assignment.

Several days later, *Time* magazine had a cover shot with an aerial view of the volcano when it had erupted. The photograph showed ash blowing to the south and the east. It was exactly what the Holy Spirit had directed me to pray. God had changed the direction of the wind! I had no way of knowing about that days before when I prayed. The Holy Spirit had revealed it to me. He is our Helper! It pays to listen and obey the Holy Spirit!

Peace Even in Trouble

When trouble comes it's the peace of God that holds us steady through it. And what keeps us in His peace is knowing that we have a covenant with Him that won't fail. If we're willing to pursue that kind of relationship with the Father, we can withstand and overcome the challenges life throws at us. We can enjoy a life filled with the peace that passes human understanding no matter what's going on around us.

As Dennis and I discovered, we can even be at peace and overcome when we're faced with a volcanic ash storm! To do so though, we must keep our focus on God and His Word. We can't get all upset about the circumstances. Had I gotten stressed and worried about that situation in Paris, it would've been nearly impossible for me to hear God's direction through the static of my fretfulness. I would have been miserably worried instead of being in faith and at peace.

Under the Umbrella

Peace is not determined by conditions around us. It's determined by the condition *within*.

It's like we're under an umbrella. First designed to protect people from the sun, the umbrella derived its name from the Latin word for shade, which is *umbra*. When we're abiding in the secret place in our position in Christ, we're under God's umbra, or shadow. Because we're in Him, we're carrying around our own personal umbrella of His influence and protection.

Everywhere we go, we have His shade of influence surrounding us and overshadowing the situations we're involved in. As long as we stay under it, His influence will empower us to stand strong in the face of conflicts, negative reports, threats to our well-being, or any other move Satan may make against us.

God's Goodness

Some people believe God brings tests and trials into their lives. But that's not the picture the Bible portrays. It describes our Lord as a good Shepherd, One worthy of our trust. It depicts Him as a Protector who only desires *good* things for us.

Psalm 23 says the Lord makes us to lie in pastures that are green—not parched. He leads us besides still waters—not raging rapids. When our minds are over-burdened with care, He restores peace to our souls.

Even when walking *through* the valley of the shadow of death, we don't have to fear, because God Almighty will see us through the valley into victory. He isn't the one who leads us into the valley, but if we're in it, He is there to lead us out!

This psalm ends with the promise: "Surely goodness and unfailing love will pursue me all the days of my life, and I will live in the house of the Lord forever."[56]

The Hebrew word for *goodness* refers to *good things, benefits, welfare, happiness and prosperity*. Those are the things

God brings us. He sends benefits and blessings to overtake us, not tests and trials.

The Bible is full of scriptures that reveal God as being good, and the devil as being evil. In fact, Psalm 92:15 makes the bold declaration, "There is nothing but goodness in him!" How anybody who reads God's Word can put the responsibility for calamity and destruction on Him, I'll never understand. Jesus settled the issue in John 10:10 when He said, "The thief's purpose is to steal and kill and destroy. My purpose is to give them a rich and satisfying life."

God is Good...All the Time

How much clearer does it need to be? God is not a thief. He sent His Son with the purpose of giving life in all its fullness. Satan is the thief. He's the author of evil. He's the one referred to in the Bible as the deceiver, the devourer, the devil, the father of lies, the destroyer, and the accuser.

None of those traits describe God. What would draw anyone to serve a God who brings sickness, disease and calamity upon His children? People have enough trouble already, why would anybody want a God who would give them even more? They wouldn't. The Bible says it's the goodness of God that leads people to repentance.[57]

God wants to demonstrate His goodness in your life so when the world sees it, they'll be drawn to Him. He wants people to know that, "Every good gift and every perfect gift is

98

from above, and comes down from the Father," as James 1:17 declares.[58]

He wants such an abundance of good things, benefits, welfare, happiness, and prosperity to overtake you that people watch you and marvel. They'll listen and believe you when you say, "Your goodness is so great! You have stored up great blessings for those who honor you. You have done so much for those who come to you for protection, blessing them before the watching world."[59]

God is so good to His children and He wants them to know it. He said so Himself, "I know the plans that I have for you...plans for welfare and not for calamity to give you a future and a hope."[60]

God Re-wove Joseph's Life

One person in the Bible whose life clearly proved this was Joseph. God launched His good plan in Joseph's life by giving him a dream. It laid out the strategy that would not only sustain his family and nation through seven years of drought but make them wealthy in the process. It revealed to Joseph his God-ordained destiny and prepared him to walk it out.

When Joseph told the dream to his brothers, however, they got jealous of him. Their hearts were filled with such hatred that they sold him as a slave, and he was carried away to Egypt.

In Egypt, Joseph went to work for a wealthy landowner named Potiphar. He managed the whole estate and everything prospered and flourished. Then Potiphar's wife lied about Joseph and he was thrown into prison.

Some people say God caused that to happen. They claim He was behind the bad things that happened to Joseph and back it up by pointing to Genesis 50:20. There, Joseph said to his brothers, "You meant evil against me, but God meant it for good in order to bring about this present result, to preserve many people alive." *Vine's Expository Dictionary of Biblical Words* says the word *meant* can be translated weave. It can be translated like this: "You thought evil against me, but God wove it for good."

Joseph knew the whole time that God was on his side, that He was weaving even what the devil meant for harm into His good plan. That's why Joseph didn't get discouraged and give up during the hard times. He trusted God. He believed through it all that God would deliver him and fulfill his dream.

David believed the same thing when he faced trying times in his life. He fought off discouragement by meditating on the goodness of the Lord. David's faith in God's goodness renewed his strength when his supply had run dry. He said, "I would have despaired unless I had believed that I would see the goodness of the Lord in the land of the living."[61]

What is it that makes *you* despair? Look to the goodness of God and it will sustain you! It will bring you through any kind of trouble into triumph.

God's Goodness Transcends Evil

Another hero in the Bible who caught hold of this revelation was Moses. He had a marvelous relationship with God. He asked God for one favor after another, and God just kept giving them to him. The more God granted his requests, the more Moses asked.

Finally, in Exodus 33:18, Moses asked the Lord, "Please, show me Your glory."[62] How did God answer? He said, "I will make all My goodness pass before you, and I will proclaim the name of the Lord before you."[63] In other words, God equated His glory and divine nature with His goodness. He revealed to Moses that they are inseparable.

This not only says something about God, it says something about us as believers. We're partakers of His divine nature. [64] God manifests His glory and identity through us. That means we're to give expression to His goodness. We're to let it flow through us to others. For as Galatians 5:22-23 says, "The fruit of the Spirit is love, joy, peace, patience, kindness, *goodness*, faithfulness, gentleness, and self-control."

The goodness of God abides within all of us who make Jesus Christ our Lord. But for it to manifest fully in our lives it must be exercised like a muscle, developed and strengthened.

Exercise isn't always fun, but it's necessary and rewarding. So, in addition to receiving God's goodness, determine to develop it every day and work it from the inside out.

Share God's goodness with others. Tell them how he has blessed you—about the benefits of serving our good, good God. And tell them when He has protected you.

The Issue Is the Heart

In Proverbs 4:23, God gives a strict charge to "keep (guard) your heart with all diligence."[65] The word *keep* means "to hedge about, guard, protect and attend to." It paints the picture of what Adam was supposed to do in the Garden of Eden. Genesis 2:15 says he was "to tend and keep it."

Adam's job, in other words, was to be watchful of anything that might threaten his garden. He was to post a guard to keep out all intruders.

That's just what we're supposed to do for our hearts. We're to watch over what goes into them by monitoring what comes through the gateways of our eyes and ears. We're to protect them from strategies of the enemy who is always seeking to steal from us.

The job of keeping your heart is a top priority! For, as Proverbs 4:23 says, "out of it spring the issues of life." When you have a well-kept heart, it continually flows with life-giving issues like health, joy, peace and love. When you let your heart get cluttered with concerns and distractions, the flow of those life-giving issues begins to dry up.

This is why maintaining your peace is so important. Like a soldier guards a city to keep out enemies and intruders, peace guards over your heart. But it can only do its job when you put your faith in God and refuse to get worried and upset about things.

Philippians 4:6-7 says, "Do not fret or have any anxiety about anything, but in every circumstance and in everything, by prayer and petition (definite requests), with thanksgiving, continue to make your wants known to God. And God's peace...which transcends all understanding shall garrison and mount guard over your hearts and minds in Christ Jesus."[66]

When you pray over everything instead of fretting, you're putting your trust in God and His Word. You're setting yourself up to walk in the fulfillment of Proverbs 3:5-6. It says, "Trust in the Lord with all your heart; and do not depend on your own understanding. Seek his will in all you do, and he will show you which paths to take."

God's straight paths are protected paths. But if you want to walk on them your trust cannot be in your understanding or ability to fix a situation; it must be in God's Word. He wants you to build faith on Him and His Word in every area of your life.

DON'T SHRINK BACK

In October of 2017, Dennis flew to Ireland where he was scheduled to speak in several churches. After his meetings in Ballymena, he was scheduled to drive to Dublin the next morning. When the pastor driving him to Dublin arrived at the hotel, he informed Dennis that hurricane Ophelia which had developed near the Azores in Portugal had reached the southern part of Ireland, headed straight for them.

Warm-water hurricanes seldom ever veer that far north.

This one was different.

Dennis texted me about the hurricane and the warning to take shelter. "I can't," he said. "I have an assignment from the Lord to preach." (If the Lord had told him to take shelter, he would have obeyed. But since He hadn't, Dennis chose to fulfill his God-given assignment in Ireland.)

Fierce storms didn't stop Jesus from fulfilling His assignment. Once while crossing the lake, high winds caused waves to break over the boat. When the disciples woke Jesus up, He rebuked the wind and spoke to the waves saying, "Peace. Be still!"[67]

While Dennis prepared for his meeting, I prayed Psalm 91:9-11, "If you make the LORD your refuge, if you make the Most High your shelter, no evil will conquer you; no plague will come near your home. For he will order his angels to protect you wherever you go."

Ophelia was regarded as the worst storm to hit Ireland in more than fifty years and was the easternmost Atlantic major hurricane on record.

News reports were alarming. "Massive destruction has fallen over Ireland: at least three people have died, gale force winds left more than 360,000 homes without power, large and destructive waves reached the coast and forecasters warned of flying debris. Winds of 119 miles per hour hit southwest Ireland."

Fearless

In the midst of it all, I knew better than to become fearful. The Bible describes fear as a spirit, and I couldn't afford to give that spirit any place. Besides, I'd learned to trust the Lord when I prayed according to His Word.

I took my stand on God's Word and refused to budge.

Dennis made it to his meeting just fine.

If Ophelia wasn't enough, the next day, a second hurricane hit. The media warned residents not to drive along the east coast because the surge of water could be treacherous. Dennis had to drive two hours along that coastal road to get to his next meeting. While he drove, I watched the storm on a radar app. It was right over him! I sent him a text.

Me: The radar indicates your about to drive into the worst of the hurricane.

Dennis: It's not even raining.

Me: The eye of the storm should be over you right now.

Dennis: Safe under the shelter of the Almighty.

Dennis drove right through that hurricane with a huge umbrella covering him—under the shadow of the Almighty. He fulfilled the assignment God had given him without any disruption.

These days, fear and anxiety have pierced many people to the depths of their being. People everywhere are searching desperately for something unshakable and immovable, to alleviate their anxieties.

Those of us who are Christians, however, shouldn't give an inch to fear or anxiety. Instead, we should evoke the courage and confidence that comes from faith in God's Word. So what if we're living in a dangerous time, like no other in history? That should simply inspire us to communicate the plan and purpose of God without reservation. To tell people about His plan for redemption and deliverance. His plan for protection.

Live by Faith

Now is not the time for believers to shrink back! Dennis's story might have had a very different ending if he had shrunk back in fear in the face of those storms. But he didn't. He forged ahead because he understood that God has given us the answers the world needs. That He has not only called us to stand in faith for our own situations, but to help others through theirs.

Hebrews 10:36-38 says the righteous—those who have been made right with God—shall live by faith. It also says God finds no pleasure in those who pull back. That's why many years ago the Lord raised up a new generation of ministers to teach the Body of Christ how to operate by faith.

Sadly, not all believers have embraced that teaching. Some listened for a while and then abandoned the message of faith in favor of a newer or more popular revelation. Many, pre-suming it was a get-rich-quick scheme, missed its purpose altogether. Others went to the extreme of claiming that the faith message has passed away.

Talk about a silly claim! According to Hebrews 11:6, "without faith it is impossible to please God." So God could never dismiss faith teaching. To do that, He'd have to cut scriptures out of the Bible.

No, God has brought faith to the forefront and He's kept it there in our day for very good reason. He wants believers to learn how to stand in faith no matter what happens around us. He wants us to learn how to live by faith, to become established and skillful enough in it to overcome every attack, because it's going to take faith to survive in these perilous days.

I know I've already said this, but it's worth saying again: The Bible warns that the closer we get to the end times, the more perils we're going to face in this world. But faith in God's Word is all-inclusive. It will protect us from them all.

It will protect us from calamity, save us from financial ruin, make us immune to biological warfare, and even shelter us from crazy weather. It will be our rock and our fortress in every storm and make us so unshakable we'll never have to shrink back in fear.

A Decision is Required

"But Vikki," you might say, "my faith just isn't that strong!"

It can be. All you have to do is keep developing it. Just make an unwavering decision to trust God's Word as the final authority in your life. Then keep planting the seed of that Word in your heart and nurturing it. Small faith can grow into great faith when studied and practiced on a regular basis.

As your faith grows, you'll start reacting differently when you're confronted with dangerous situations. You'll remember Isaiah 60:2 promises that when darkness increases in the earth the glory of God will rest upon you. You'll remember God can be trusted to take care of those who believe Him. As Hosea 6:3 says, "He will respond to us as surely as the arrival of dawn or the coming of rains in early spring."

Notice, according to that verse, God's response to our faith is as predictable as the laws of nature. We can count on Him to perform His Word in our life just as surely as we can count on the seasons to change and the sun to come up in the morning.

Do you ever worry about the seasons getting stuck or the sun failing to rise? No, you expect them to keep following the pattern they've followed ever since creation. You can have the same kind of expectancy when it comes to God's promises of protection. You can count on the fact that He *will* respond to those who trust in His unfailing Word.

God Protected Jesus

Jesus' life was a demonstration of living under God's protective care. On multiple occasions, angry people tried to kill Him, but they couldn't because He put His trust in God's ability to keep Him safe. Only when His mission on earth had been fulfilled, and He chose to lay down His life, was the enemy able to touch Him.

Jesus' life serves to teach us how to live in greater degrees of God's protection. He set the example so that we can live in safety and finish our assignment on earth, too. For us to do so though, we must get to know and trust God like Jesus did.

Is that really possible? Can we actually live like Jesus did and experience the same results?

Yes! In John 14:12, He said, "I tell you the truth, anyone who believes in me will do the same works I have done, and even greater works, because I am going to be with the Father." In addition, Daniel 11:32 declares, "But the people who know their God shall be strong and do great things."[68]

When you put those two verses together you can see the key to doing greater works is found in two words: *believe* and *know* God. You don't have to know *how* God will protect or deliver you; what's important is believing and knowing He *will*.

Trust the Shepherd

In John 10, Jesus compared Himself with a protective, watchful, affectionate shepherd, and described us as His sheep. He said:

> The sheep hear his voice; and he calls his own sheep by name and leads them out. And when he brings out his own sheep, he goes before them; and the sheep follow him, for they know his voice...I am the good shepherd; and I know My sheep, and am known by My own. [69]

It's wonderful to realize that Jesus knows your thoughts, intentions, desires, and circumstances. But it's even more amazing to think that you can know His thoughts, His intentions, and desires. That you can follow Him because you know and hear His voice.

One of the ways a shepherd keeps his sheep safe is by talking to them. He speaks to them constantly, so they become familiar with his voice and rely on Him for protection and guidance. Similarly, Jesus constantly speaks to us as believers. As we listen to Him, we learn to recognize His voice and depend on Him to lead us in safety even when we're surrounded by danger.

Of course, to benefit from what He says to us we must maintain an obedient heart. Hearing His voice doesn't do much good if we don't follow Him and do what He tells us to do.

King David was a shepherd, so he grasped this better than most. He knew from experience that the safety of his sheep depended not only on their knowing him but on their obedience to him as well. He also had great confidence that God, as his Shepherd, had the ability to protect him in the most treacherous situation. He said it time and again in his writings:

- Now I know that the Lord saves His anointed; He will answer him from His holy heaven, with the saving strength of His right hand.[70]

- I know that the Lord will maintain the cause of the afflicted, and justice for the poor. [71]

- Then my enemies will turn back...this I know, God is for me.[72]

- And those who know Your name will put their trust in You; for You, Lord, have not forsaken those who seek You.[73]

Unlike David, many believers tend to depend on their own limited knowledge and unreliable ability to get through tough times. But that's a mistake. Especially in our day, circumstances are likely to arise that are beyond the most powerful individual's ability to control. Taking a self-reliant approach to such situations is sure to end in disaster.

Wise believers know there is a greater power available to them. They've abandoned reliance on their own incompetent ways to embrace the insight and power of the almighty, all-knowing God.

These believers refuse to allow fear to enter in and cause them to detour from God's purpose and plan for their lives. They won't change course—even if confronted with a hurricane in Ireland. They won't shrink back. They've discovered that trusting in the Lord and His ability to save and protect is what will ensure their success.

EARS TO HEAR
AND EYES TO SEE

I turned off the news with a sigh, weary of hearing about so many terrorists with no regard for life. They killed themselves and multitudes of others across America and around the world. I had no frame of reference for such a culture of death, except that the Bible had warned us of these dangerous days.

I walked to the laundry room to get a load of towels out of the dryer. As I did, I glanced out the window and paused. It was one thing to see terrorists on the news. It was another to suspect they might live across the street.

Of course, I didn't have any solid proof. What I did have was dozens of small incidents that had morphed into full blown suspicion. I didn't know the man who lived in the house across the street. But I couldn't shake the sense that something wasn't right.

What troubled me most was the frequency of the meetings that were held there. Sometimes several men drove to the house. Others arrived on foot, leading me to believe that they also lived in our neighborhood. I'd never seen a woman there.

In February 2011, a plot to bomb the Dallas home of former President George W. Bush was revealed and thwarted. A 20-year-old Saudi student was arrested. The day after that story broke, there was another meeting of the men across the street. I knew it was strategic.

The windows on my neighbor's house were covered, blinds shut. The place appeared as locked down as Fort Knox. I'd considered reporting it, but I had no more than suspicions. I mentioned to Dennis that I thought it was strange.

On a motorcycle vacation with several friends, I told them what I'd seen.

"Have you called the FBI?" my friend asked.

"No."

"Did you know we have an FBI agent who sits on the front row of our church?" another said.

The next week I went to church and I introduced myself to the agent. When I told her my story she said, "Have you called the FBI?"

"That's why I'm talking to you."

See and Say

"Here's the deal," she said. "When you see something; say something. My sister lives in Florida and the day after 911 she called and told me that her neighbor had packed up and disappeared without warning three days earlier. She thought it odd, but she didn't say anything. He piloted the jet that flew into the North Tower on 9/11."

She gave my name and number to an FBI agent to contact me. "When you talk to him, less is better," she explained. "Tell him what you've observed. How many cars? How many men? How often do they meet? After you report it, it will be an open investigation, so you won't hear anything back. Stay out of it."

I reported what I'd seen to the FBI agent.

A short time later Dennis came home and announced, "There's a police car parked outside the gate to our street and another one outside the neighbor's house across the street." Their presence remained for two weeks.

After the police presence disappeared, so did my neighbor. He'd left in the middle of the night. It took a year for the house to be repaired from all the damage before it could be lived in again. The new owner said, "There is so much coaxial cable in the attic, that there's no way to get rid of it all."

This is just a reminder of why we must have eyes to see; both in the natural realm and in the spirit realm.

A Gift From the Lord

Our natural five physical senses can't pick up on everything God wants to reveal to us. So, to alert us to things that in the physical world are being kept under cover, He's given us a better way to perceive them. He's given us spiritual senses we can use to pick up on whatever we need to know. As Proverbs 20:12 says, "Ears to hear and eyes to see—both are gifts from the Lord."

The definition of the Hebrew word *see* in that verse includes being able to perceive and discern. The meaning of the word *hear* includes the ability to receive and understand a supernatural revelation. So that verse is not just talking about the natural capacity to see and hear that God has given us. It's referring to the ability He's given us to see and hear in the spirit.

If you didn't have that ability, you'd be extremely limited. You'd be what the New Testament calls a "natural man." According to First Corinthians 2:14, "The natural man does not receive the things of the Spirit of God, for they are foolishness to him; nor can he know them, because they are spiritually discerned."[74]

That's a dangerous condition to be in for two reasons. First, the natural realm of the senses is where Satan governs. He can easily deceive and hide things from people who operate only in that realm. Second, because God is a Spirit, sense-ruled

118

people can't know Him in a deep, intimate way. They can't receive and benefit from His wisdom.

As a believer, however, you're not in this condition! You're not a natural man. You aren't limited to the realm of the five physical senses. You're a born-again spirit being. You've turned your life over to Jesus and been made alive to God, so you can know Him and the hidden mysteries of the spirit.

Rather than living your life according to the fleshly "mind of the senses," which Romans 8:6 says, "is death," you can live your life with your "mind set on the Spirit which is life and peace."[75] You can live continually receiving from God "the Spirit of wisdom and of revelation in the knowledge of him... having the eyes of your hearts enlightened, so that you may know...."[76]

Look again at those verses. How do they say spiritual knowledge comes to you? Through "the eyes of your heart." That means your heart, or recreated spirit, can see into the realm where God lives; it can hear from the realm where God speaks. Your spirit can perceive things that are hidden from the natural senses and receive illumination, increased knowledge, and understanding directly from God.

Many Christians have believed that only ministers can do this. That only prophets and apostles have this kind of spiritual perception. But these verses in Ephesians contradict such notions. Written by Paul under the inspiration of the Holy Spirit, they were addressed to believers not just to ministers, and they say all of us can have the eyes of our heart enlightened and receive spiritual revelation. In fact, it's essential to our understanding of spiritual matters. Without it, no one can comprehend the things of God.

Open His Eyes that He Might See

Accounts of men and women hearing and seeing into the spirit realm fill both the Old and the New Testaments. But one of the most interesting is in Second Kings 6. It tells about a time when the king of Syria was at war with Israel and his plans kept getting frustrated. Every time his soldiers attacked, it turned out the Israelites had been tipped off beforehand.

Initially, he thought there was a traitor or a spy in his camp, but one of his servants told him that wasn't the case. "It's not us, my lord the king," one of the officers replied. "Elisha, the prophet in Israel, tells the king of Israel even the words you speak in the privacy of your bedroom!"[77]

To solve the problem, the king ordered that Elisha be captured. He sent horses and chariots and a great army to track him down in the night. The next morning Elisha's servant woke up to find they were surrounded by Syrian troops. Overcome with fear he cried out, "Oh, sir, what will we do now?"

"Don't be afraid!" Elisha told him. "For there are more on our side than on theirs!" Then Elisha prayed, "O Lord, open his eyes and let him see!"[78] We know that the physical eyes of the servant were already open, because he had seen the Syrian forces. So obviously Elisha wasn't praying for him to be able to see in the natural. He was praying for him to see in the spirit.

Sure enough, the Lord granted Elisha's request. He opened the servant's spiritual eyes and when He did the servant saw that the mountains around them were full of horses and chariots of fire. He saw the host of angels that accompanied them in the spirit realm, of which he'd been unaware.

You may not realize it, but we as Christians have angels accompanying us too. Hebrews 1:14 calls them "servants—spirits sent to care for people who will inherit salvation." Angels have an assignment from God—to render service for you and me. But many believers neglect to take advantage of their assistance. They struggle without the supernatural intervention of angels because, like Elisha's servant, they're unaware their angels are even there.

That's a sad state of affairs! Angels can bring great things to pass. They're sent by the Lord; they "excel in strength, who do His word, Heeding the voice of His word."[79] Angels are willing and able to do whatever God instructs. They're mighty and well qualified for the work.

Even now, they're standing ready, waiting to hear us speak God's Word. When they do, they won't dispute or delay. They'll spring into action and execute our commands of faith.

If You Believe You Will See

"But if all this is true," somebody might say, "if we as God's people really do have spiritual eyes and ears, why aren't we seeing and hearing more in that realm?"

Primarily because we haven't believed to do so. Or, if we have, we've believed only to a limited degree. Some people, for instance, have believed to *hear* but have been hesitant to *see* in the spirit for fear of being deceived. You need not worry about being deceived if what you see agrees with the Word of God. So, don't settle for hearing only. Press in with your faith for revelation to understand hidden mysteries.

Jesus promised in John 11:40 that "you would see God's glory if you believe." So, stand on that promise. You had to believe to receive salvation. You have to believe to receive healing and finances. It only makes sense that the same applies to the operation of your spiritual senses. So, begin to use your faith to move into a realm of seeing and knowing.

That's what King David did. In Psalm 27:13, he expressed his desperation to see. He said, "I had fainted, unless I had believed to see the goodness of the Lord in the land of the living."[80] Unless he had believed to see something, David wouldn't have made it through.

Much of the same is true for us as believers. In Christ, we have available to us everything we need to make it through every situation, but it's not all visible in this natural realm. If we want to see it and access it, we must do it by faith. We must

122

tap into the spiritual realm by the power of the Holy Spirit within us. For, as First Corinthians 2 says:

> It is written: "Eye has not seen, nor ear heard, nor have entered into the heart of man the things which God has prepared for those who love Him." But God has revealed them to us through His Spirit. For the Spirit searches all things, yes, the deep things of God. For what man knows the things of a man except the spirit of the man which is in him? Even so no one knows the things of God except the Spirit of God. Now we have received, not the spirit of the world, but the Spirit who is from God, that we might know the things that have been freely given to us by God.[81]

God has all kinds of things to show you that cannot be discovered through your physical senses. They include everything from angels on assignment to hidden dangers in your neighborhood, and they can only be discovered by the light of revelation. You *can* see, hear and conceive them, but only by supernatural manifestation of the Spirit.

Jesus said, "Everything that the Father has is Mine...He [the Spirit] will take the things that are Mine and will reveal (declare, disclose, transmit) it to you."[82] So, believe it and expect the Holy Spirit to do His job. He will reveal the things of the spirit to you. He's so committed to it, in fact, He'll use any means possible—reveal, declare, disclose, transmit—or download them. He might even show you something that needs to be reported to the FBI.

The Mystery Revealed

Receiving such revelation from the Holy Spirit isn't automatic though. You will have to do your part. You'll have to give Him the opportunity to speak to you, and one way you can do so is by praying in other tongues.

In the lives of the first disciples, praying in tongues made all the difference. Before they could pray in tongues, they didn't have much revelation at all. Even though they spent three years ministering with Jesus, they had almost no understanding of His mission on earth. They thought He'd come to restore the natural nation of Israel…and they continued to think so even after He rose from the dead.[83]

After they were filled with the Holy Spirit on the Day of Pentecost and spoke with other tongues, however, their spiritual eyes were opened. Peter suddenly began to preach that Jesus had come to provide "the remission of sins and…the gift of the Holy Spirit. For the promise is to you and to your children," he said, "and to all who are afar off, as many as the Lord our God will call."[84]

Isn't that amazing? After three years of missing the point, as soon as the Holy Spirit came upon the disciples and they spoke in tongues, they got the revelation. The Holy Spirit unveiled to them the mystery that had been hidden.

If we'll pray in tongues, we too can have insight into mysteries. For as First Corinthians 14:2 says, "One who speaks in a tongue does not speak to men, but to God; for no one understands, but in his spirit he speaks mysteries."[85] The word *mystery* means the hidden thing, a secret, the secret counsel of God. It refers not only to great redemptive truths, such as the plan of salvation, but to secrets God has hidden from the kingdom of darkness, and to the revelation and enlightenment we need for our everyday lives.

The Holy Spirit knows what lies ahead, and part of His ministry is to show you what's to come. Praying in tongues helps you tap into that revelation. It helps you pick up in advance on what the devil may be planning and causes the hidden, secret plans of God to be revealed and set in motion in your life.

Jesus said to His followers, "To you it has been granted to know the mystery of the kingdom of heaven."[86] But you cannot know the hidden mysteries of the kingdom with your natural senses. You can only know them as you perceive what God is revealing to you in the spirit.

So, take the time to develop yourself spiritually. Discipline your flesh (this does take discipline because the flesh always wars against the spirit) and press into the spirit realm in a deeper way. Spend time every day praying in tongues.

One of these days, you'll be very glad you did.

PROTECTION FOR OUR FAMILIES

The day Veronica Bailey[87] met her daughter's boyfriend, Danny, spiritual alarms wailed like a tornado warning. The Holy Spirit revealed the danger to Veronica.

"Jennifer," Veronica warned when they were alone, "I know you won't like hearing this, but there's a spirit of abuse on Danny."

"Oh, Mom...."

She didn't believe it and dismissed her mother's concerns.

Jennifer was a smart girl, loved the Lord and usually made good decisions. She'd been raised in a Christian home and had no frame of reference for true domestic abuse.

Her mothers' warnings fell on deaf ears.

One day, Veronica saw Danny kick at their little defense-less dog while sitting in their family room and spoke up, "Don't ever kick my dog again."

Danny just laughed and said, "We have a Doberman pincher and all my dad has to do is touch his belt buckle and he cowers."

Later that evening, Veronica brought the incident up wondering if Jennifer had heard Danny's comment. "Does it bother you that Danny's dog cowers when his father touches his belt? Evidently, the dog knows a belt can cause pain. I've read that some very dangerous people get their start by abusing animals."

"Mom, you're blowing this out of proportion," Jennifer insisted.

"Then promise me one thing," Veronica asked. "Promise me that when he hits you, you'll call 911."

Jennifer rolled her eyes and sighed. Before long, she'd moved into her own apartment.

Danny turned on the charm, as abusive men sometimes do. He also took control of Jennifer's phone when she was with him. One small step at a time, he began isolating her from family and friends. He wanted to have complete control of her life.

Fight From a Spiritual Position

Veronica had a friend whose daughter had been caught in a similar unhealthy relationship, except they'd had a child. In a conversation with her friend, Veronica asked, "Tell me everything you did right and everything you did wrong while dealing with the situation." Veronica knew it wasn't as much what her friend would say, but the wisdom and direction the Lord would speak to her during this conversation.

"Every time he comes to pick up his son," Veronica's friend explained, "he has a defiant smirk on his face as though he's mocking me. I always pray that I won't react, but as soon as I see that smirk it goes all over me. I get so upset that I have to leave the room and pray."

Right then the Lord spoke to Veronica warning, "*If you try to fight this spiritual battle while you're emotional, you'll lose. The enemy will win because he works in the physical realm, playing on your emotions. To fight a spirit, you must fight in the spirit. There's no room for emotions.*"

Veronica could see it was true. But how was she supposed to take control of her emotions? The Lord took her to Second Corinthians 10:3-5:

For though we walk in the flesh, we do not war according to the flesh (for the weapons of our warfare are not of the flesh, but mighty before God to the casting down of strongholds); casting down imaginations, and every high thing that is exalted against the knowledge of God, and *bringing every thought into captivity to the obedience of Christ.*[88]

Reading those verses, Veronica realized she had fallen headfirst into fear. She was afraid for her daughter's safety, and her thoughts were like a runaway train. They were flitting from one fearful scenario to another, keeping her emotions in a state of turmoil. So, the first step to getting her emotions under control was for her to take her fearful thoughts captive.

Instead of imaging the worst possible outcome, Veronica had to make a change. She had to bring her thoughts into the obedience of Christ, making them submit to God's Word.

The Lord impressed her to face each of her fears and conquer them with the Word. It was no small feat and it led to some of the most intense times of her life. Each night while in bed Veronica faced one of her fears, allowing the Lord to lead her out of fear into faith through His wonderful promises.

Knowing Danny was abusive, Veronica stared that fear in the face. *What if he abused her?*

The idea of Jennifer suffering made Veronica cry out to God. As soon as Jennifer began dating Danny, the Lord had instructed Veronica and her husband to pray many of the verses from Jeremiah 31. Although these verses referred to Israel, they're just as applicable to Jennifer's situation. Verses 10-12 assured her the Lord "…will gather them together and watch over them as a shepherd does his flock. For the Lord has redeemed Israel [Jennifer] from those too strong for them. They will come home and sing songs of joy...."

The fear lifted and joy filled Veronica's heart until she laughed out loud. She was confident the Lord would not only watch over Jennifer but deliver her from Danny's influence.

The next night, Veronica faced another horrific thought. *What if he raped her and she became pregnant?* She felt the raw emotions that stemmed from such a perverse act. The Lord instructed Veronica to pray that Jennifer's reproductive system would "stand still" until she was free from Danny's control. At first that sounded crazy. She had never heard of anyone praying like that. But the Holy Spirit reminded her of what Joshua had done during one battle.

> On the day the Lord gave the Israelites victory over the Amorites, Joshua prayed to the Lord in front of all the people of Israel. He said, "Let the sun stand still over Gibeon, and the moon over the Valley of Aijalon." So the sun and the moon stood still until the Israelites had defeated their enemies.[89]

Once the Holy Spirit had given Veronica a scriptural foundation, she began to pray and speak those words over Jennifer's reproductive system.

What if he abducted her and I never saw her again? The pain of even considering this was excruciating. Again, Veronica found comfort from Jeremiah 31. "But now the Lord says, 'Do not weep any longer, for I will reward you. Your children will come back to you from the distant land of the enemy.'"[90] These verses removed the fear that tried to suffocate Veronica. The Lord had promised that Jennifer would come home!

Consequently, He gave Veronica several instructions to help Jennifer find her way home. "Set up road signs; put up guideposts. Mark well the path by which you came. Come back again, my virgin Israel [Jennifer]; return to your cities here. How long will you wander, my wayward daughter? For the Lord will cause something new and different to happen— Israel [Jennifer] will embrace her God." [91]

Veronica wept, not from fear, but from the relief and confidence these promises gave her. When she read verse 36 and 37, they expressed exactly the way she felt about Jennifer. They said, "I am as likely to reject my people Israel [Jennifer] as I am to do away with the laws of nature! Just as the heavens cannot be measured and the foundation of the earth cannot be explored, so I will not consider casting them away forever for their sins. I, the Lord, have spoken!"

Night after agonizing night, scenario after heartrending scenario, Veronica had confronted the possible plans the devil had for Jennifer. She had wept until there were no more tears. The Lord had ministered to her through His Word until fear had lost its power.

Ready for Battle

Veronica climbed out of bed after dealing with each fear feeling invincible. She'd faced down every fear and not a shred of anxiety or dreadful emotion remained. She'd expected to feel hollow and empty after all those tears, but the opposite was true. She'd defeated fear and runaway emotions with God's promises and by her authority in His Name. She stood strong on such a solid foundation of faith that she felt like a warrior wearing a suit of armor.

"You've gotten rid of the fear that crippled your faith," the Lord said. *"Now you're equipped to fight...so FIGHT!"*

Veronica stepped into the kitchen and announced, "Devil, somebody's going down and it won't be me or my daughter!"

The enemy had used Danny to try and destroy and detour Jennifer's life and destiny.

It wasn't going to happen.

Veronica went to war with relentless intensity. She clamped her spiritual jaws on that assignment against her daughter and nothing could make her let go.

Sowing Seed for a Miracle

Twice during that time, Veronica heard the Lord say, *"Give an offering of $1,000 as seed for Jennifer's freedom."*

She didn't tell anyone about that. She realized that a lot of Christians would think she was trying to buy a miracle. Not so.

Spirit-led giving was a way of life for Veronica and her husband. She'd always strived to be quick to obey whatever she heard the Lord say. She also understood that when a miracle is needed, to bring it forth God often asks for our participation.

In First Kings 17, for instance, the widow of Zarephath needed a miracle during a famine. She had only enough oil left to make one loaf of bread for herself and her son. Her plan was to eat it and die.

But God had a different plan.

He instructed His prophet, Elijah, to ask her to make that loaf for *him*. She obeyed the word of the Lord and gave her last meal to Elijah. Afterward, God gave her such a supernatural supply of oil that she and her son had enough to eat until the famine was over.

Did that woman buy a miracle with her loaf of bread? No, she proved that she would trust and obey God despite the circumstances. And He honored her faith.

Veronica's situation was similar in that God had asked her to do something to engage her faith. The money He asked her to give was nothing compared to what He'd asked of the widow. Veronica gave from her abundance; the widow gave all she had.

The third time it happened, Veronica was in a meeting when the minister said, "Anybody who'll give $1,000 will receive a miracle in seven days. Come forward now."

A miracle in seven days sounded like a slice of heaven. About thirty or forty people responded, but Veronica beat all of them to the front of the church.

"For two of you," the minister added, "this is about your children."

Veronica gave $1,000 and *knew* she had her miracle.

Seven days from that night would be the following Monday. Back home, she sent Jennifer a text. *How about I take you to dinner next Monday night?*

Jennifer seemed okay with the invitation and agreed to meet her mother on Monday.

Except when the appointed hour arrived, Jennifer didn't. Veronica had no anxiety. Her emotions stayed calm. She had no idea why Jennifer didn't show up, but she was fully persuaded she had received her miracle.

The next day, Jennifer told her mother what had happened.

"Danny stopped by while I was getting ready to meet you for dinner," Jennifer explained. "He stepped in the door, saw the keys in my purse, snatched them and left. When I tried to stop him, he knocked me down onto the concrete and I hit my head. That's when I remembered your words: 'When he hits you, call 911.' That's what I did."

When a female police officer showed up, she asked Jennifer what had happened. Then she said, "You need to press charges."

"He told me that he's so sorry when he loses his temper," Jennifer said.

"Yes," the officer replied, "and he'll be *sorry* when he kills you." That convinced Jennifer to press charges. Danny was arrested and taken to jail.

God rescued Jennifer on Monday, the seventh day, just like God spoke through that minister.

Trust God's Goodness

In these perilous days, none of us want anything more than to see our children and families safe and serving the Lord. So, it's wonderful to know God has included them in His plan. It's comforting to realize that, even while Satan is roaming around like a roaring lion seeking whom he may devour, we can trust the Lord to protect those nearest and dearest to us.

It's no wonder the psalmist said to Him, "Your goodness is so great! You have stored up great blessings for those who honor you. You have done so much for those who come to you for protection, blessing them before the watching world."[92]

God has given us promises we can stand on even for family members who aren't yet born again!

In Acts 16:31, for instance, He promises, "...Believe in the Lord Jesus and you will be saved, along with everyone in your household." That's right—until our unsaved relatives surrender their lives to God, we can make sure they are wrapped in His protection.

He even promises, "He will deliver one who is not innocent, and he will be delivered through the cleanness of your hands."[93] We can stand on God's Word and believe that even if they're still living their lives in rebellion they'll be delivered from all harm because of *our* obedience to His Covenant.

The Bible tells about people who did this for their families. It establishes precedent for us by mentioning several people of faith whose ungodly relatives were protected through times of disaster, war, and even terrorism. Two of those people were righteous men who had faith in God. Another believed in God but was not what we'd consider righteous and was outside of God's covenant altogether.

These three individuals cover most any situation you might face when it comes to protecting your family members. So as we look at their examples in the Word, let their accounts stir up your faith to see your family delivered and kept safe from destruction.

Noah and Abraham:
Saved from Flood and Fire

The first precedent was set with Noah. He was the only righteous man living in a generation when the wickedness of mankind had spiraled out of control. Genesis 6 says that in Noah's day, man's wickedness broke God's heart.[94] People's evil ways pushed Him to the point where He decided to send a flood to destroy everybody on the earth—except Noah, the only righteous man on earth.

Because Noah obeyed God and had a close relationship with Him, the Lord was committed to his safety. So He told Noah to build a ship large enough to hold his family and two of every kind of animal. Then He made a powerful commitment to him. He said, "I will confirm my covenant with you. So enter the boat—you and your wife and your sons and their wives."[95]

Even though Noah had no physical evidence to verify what he'd heard, he trusted God and obeyed. He set an example of steadfast faith before his family—trusting God for deliverance from unseen future destruction.

As a result, Noah's sons trusted him. They took refuge with him in the ark. So when the flood came, while the rest of the world perished, Noah's entire family was saved.

The second scriptural precedent for receiving supernatural protection for loved ones was set by Abraham. He too had a covenant with the Lord, so when the city of Sodom, where

Abraham's nephew Lot lived, was about to be destroyed the Lord told Abraham in advance. He visited Abraham's house to deliver a warning. Abraham responded by asking the Lord,

"Suppose you find fifty innocent people there within the city—will you still sweep it away and not spare it for their sakes?" The Lord replied, "If I find fifty innocent people in Sodom, I will spare the entire city for their sake."[96]

Abraham kept negotiating until the Lord agreed to spare Sodom if even ten righteous people could be found. Sadly, it turned out, ten righteous people could *not* be found there, so the city wasn't spared. But God still honored Abraham's intercession and delivered his nephew.

He sent angels to get Lot out of Sodom before the fire consumed it and what the angels said to Lot is worth noting:

"Do you have any other relatives here in the city?" they asked. "Get them out of this place—your sons-in-law, sons, daughters, or anyone else. For we are about to destroy this city completely. The outcry against this place is so great it has reached the Lord, and he has sent us to destroy it."[97]

The Lord is interested in our relatives staying safe and protected from destruction. But *we* must pray and believe for their deliverance. As we do, God will save our loved ones just as He did Lot.

God rescued Lot and he wasn't even sure he wanted to be rescued! He was so hesitant to leave Sodom that the angels who came to get him actually had to seize him by the hand and drag him out of the city before it was destroyed. Why did they do it? Not because Lot was righteous but because of the covenant Abraham had with God.

Abraham's covenant with God was so powerful that He wouldn't destroy Sodom until Lot had been delivered into a safe place. The angel made this clear. "I can do nothing, until you are there…" he said as he seized Lot's hand.[98] Only after God had fulfilled His promise to protect Abraham's family could the angel rain down fire and the wicked city be destroyed.

As believers we're partakers of Abraham's covenant.[99] Therefore, God is as committed to keeping *our* relatives from destruction as He was to delivering Abraham's—but only as we commit ourselves to pray for them. Only as we stand in the gap for our families like Noah, Abraham and Veronica did.

Our families may not consider us to be much of a blessing right now, but if they understood the power we bring to bear for their safety, they would appreciate us a lot more. They would be happy if they knew that in answer to our prayers, God will rescue them from destruction, even when they don't deserve it. As Job 22:30 says, "Even sinners will be rescued; they will be rescued because your hands are pure."

Rahab's Plan and God's Protection

Perhaps the most dramatic precedent we see in the Bible where protecting family members is concerned was set by Rahab—a harlot. Her story proves that no matter how far from God our relatives might be, He can still reach them. He's always looking for ways to bless and deliver humanity and if we'll give Him the slightest amount of faith to work with, He'll do the seemingly impossible for those we love.

Rahab lived in the day when the Israelites had just crossed the Jordan River and were preparing to conquer the land God had promised Israel. Everyone in the land had already heard about them—about how their God fought for them and defeated all their enemies—and everybody was terrified. Especially the people in Rahab's hometown of Jericho.

As the Israelites got closer, rumors spread about an impending attack and Israeli spies within the city walls. Panic seized the entire population, from the palace to the lowliest peasant. What was to become of them? Would any of them survive? The citizens of Jericho, having heard that no city thus far had been able to withstand the Israelites attacks, lost hope, and fear ran rampant. As Joshua 2:11 says, "our hearts melted in fear and everyone's courage failed because of you...."[100]

While others fainted, however, Rahab took a different attitude. Where they saw nothing but certain death, she saw a chance to change her life. So she devised a plan. Instead of fighting the invaders, she would risk everything and take their side. Even though she was a Canaanite harlot and a worshiper of Baal, she would trust in the God of Israel to save her.

Rahab knew if there were spies in the city, they'd need a place to stay for the night. A place where they could go, and nobody would ask questions. What better place than a harlot's home?

Rahab was aware, of course, that if she was caught aiding the spies, she'd be executed by the king as a traitor. But then, if she did nothing, she would die anyway. So she took a leap of faith and made a choice that would change her destiny. She hid the spies on her roof under stalks of flax.

She also struck a deal with them. She said, "Now swear to me by the Lord that you will be kind to me and my family since I have helped you. Give me some guarantee that when Jericho is conquered, you will let me live, along with my father and mother, my brothers and sisters, and all their families."[101]

The spies agreed and told their commander Joshua what they'd promised. In turn, he gave specific instructions to his army. "The city and everything in it must be completely destroyed as an offering to the Lord," he said, "only Rahab the prostitute and the others in her house will be spared, for she protected our spies."[102]

God had to perform a mighty miracle to save Rahab and her family because her house was built into the city wall!

It should have been destroyed when the wall came crashing to the ground. But it wasn't. Instead, that portion of the wall—and only that portion—was left standing. It dared not fall because God had sworn to protect the people in Rahab's home and keep them safe from danger.

If God swore to save a harlot and her relatives who didn't even have a covenant with Him, think how much more He'll do for us, His New Covenant children. If He'll exert that kind of mighty power for them, think how powerfully He'll move on our behalf!

When the battle of Jericho was over that day, from the dust of the rubble, the young men "…brought out Rahab, her father, mother, brothers, and all the other relatives who were with her. They moved her whole family to a safe place near the camp of Israel." [103]

Rahab and her family were witnesses to God's promise in Psalm 91:7-8: "A thousand may fall at your side, and ten thousand at your right hand; but it shall not come near you. Only with your eyes shall you look, and see the reward of the wicked."[104]

But that's not the end of the story.

Rahab's family also became one of the families listed in the genealogy of Jesus. According to Bible history, Rahab married one of the spies that she hid on her roof and later became the great-grandmother of King David. All because she believed God would save and protect her.

Marvelous things were accomplished through Rahab's life, because she trusted God. And as *we* trust in the Lord, He'll do marvelous things in our lives and in the lives of our family members as well.

Like Veronica, we don't have to fear the danger and traps that have been set against our children. We have God's promise of supernatural protection that we can claim for ourselves and for our loved ones in the last days. We may not know until we get to Heaven how many times our prayers have saved others from disaster. But we *can* know that we have the authority to stand in the gap for the safety and protection of our families.

ECONOMIC PROTECTION

I t was an election year, and the Lord had shown me who was going to win. He'd also told me that a difficult time would follow. A few of my friends spoke gloom and doom over the election, but I knew better. I refused to talk about it. I didn't want to use my words and my God-given authority as a believer in a damaging way.

Knowing the economy was going to take a hard hit was discouraging. I sought the Lord, and He directed me to Genesis 7:16. There, in the account of Noah's ark, the Bible says, "Those that entered, male and female of all flesh, went in as God had commanded him; and the Lord shut him in."[105]

What a wonderful place to be. Shut in and protected by God!

Noah got into that place by entering through the ark's only door. That door, which offered the only escape from the terrible flood, represents the salvation we have in Christ. He is our Ark and He said "I am the door. If anyone enters by Me, he will be saved."[106]

When Noah closed the ark's door behind him, "the Lord shut him in." By giving me that verse, the Lord was saying He'd do the same for me. He was instructing me to declare Genesis 7:16 as a promise by faith—that Dennis and I would be shut in and supernaturally protected during the economic crisis to come. So that's what I began to do.

The Lord also instructed me to do everything He'd taught me to ensure our financial safety during the upcoming recession. I supported the candidate who stood for godly values. I prayed. I gave money to the campaign as my seed for financial protection. I also worked at the election poll during early voting. I worked seven days a week from 6:30 a.m. to 7:30 p.m. for two weeks. I sowed seed in every possible way as an act of my faith for supernatural protection from the recession.

Trouble at the Polls

Election day was charged and volatile. Angry people showed up to vote, and in some instances the police had to be called. One woman arrived at the polls with her son who'd never voted. When he voluntarily handed me his ID, she flew into a rage. "You can't have his ID!" she screamed. Nothing anyone said calmed her.

A policeman arrived and tried to reason with her. "It's illegal to cause a disturbance at a polling place," he warned. She kept causing trouble but somehow managed to avoid being arrested.

Our candidate looked great in the polls, a fact that kept Dennis hopeful.

"It doesn't matter what the polls show," I said. "I'm going to sow seed so we don't get stuck in the economic aftermath."

Each time I gave an offering or my time, I prayed, "Lord, this is my seed so that we will be shut up in the ark of protection."

The election results were just what the Lord had shown me. Our candidate lost.

The next year, a severe recession hit.

Even then, I refused to speak gloom, doom or anything except God's Word over our nation and our finances. Over the next few years, lending institutions began to fail, and multiplied thousands of people lost their homes to foreclosure.

Miraculously, during the next two years our income increased by 70 percent. God gave us wisdom before the crisis hit, just like He did for Noah. Throughout that entire recession, we were blessed and prospered—our finances shut in the ark of God's protection.

Many people don't know they can trust God for economic protection, because they don't realize that's part of the salvation He's provided for us. Unaware of the provisions He's made for us in His Covenant, they can't benefit from them. They're like someone who's been left an inheritance from a rich relative and never bothered to collect it.

The Significance of the Head

Unlike many Christians, however, devout Jews don't tend to suffer from this lack of awareness. They're very familiar with the financial promises in their Covenant. They've also built into their very culture reminders that God promised them economic blessings and protection.

One of my friends noticed this when she attended an extravagant dinner in Israel with a group of Jewish friends. She said that she removed the cloche dome from her meal to find an entire fish on her plate—with head intact and dead eyes staring up at her. Why did they serve the entire head instead of just fileting the fish? It was a reminder, she was told, that God said in Deuteronomy 28 that He would make the Jews the head and not the tail. The first and not the last. Above only and never beneath.[107]

That's God's Word for us as believers today as well.

It's as much His will now to increase His people as it ever was. It's just the way He is. He's a good Father "who daily loads us with benefits, the God of our salvation!"[108]

There is a term used in economics: the miracle of compound interest. More math than miracle, it describes the amazing multiplication that takes place when interest on an investment is compounded each day. Talk about being loaded with benefits! When interest is compounded, it's applied not only to the original deposit, but also to the interest already paid. When it's added daily, the money multiplies at a tremendous rate.

That's not just an economic principle, it's a principle of God! He's always been a multiplier. When He created man, He blessed him and said, "Be fruitful, and multiply, and replenish the earth...."[109] We see the evidence of it all around us. The animal kingdom multiplies. Trees, plants, vegetables, flowers, and people multiply. Even spiritual things multiply, as the Apostle Paul made clear when he prayed for the churches to multiply in grace and peace.

God is essentially shouting to us all the time, through creation and through the Bible, that He intends for us to always be increasing—even during a recession. In the good times and the difficult times, His plan is for us to increase. For us to constantly say what the psalmist did:

> Your goodness is so great! You have stored up great blessings for those who honor you. You have done so much for those who come to you for protection, blessing them before the watching world.[110]

Notice that verse says the world is watching us. What does God want them to see? He wants them to see His goodness in our lives. He wants us to prosper so much that we become walking demonstrations of His love and generosity. He wants them to see His protection in our lives.

This is one of the reasons it's so important for God's people to experience His financial blessings—so that people in the world will see His faithfulness in our lives. So they'll be drawn to Him and put their faith in Him. Second Corinthians 3:2 says our lives are an epistle written for all men to read. God wants people to read the letter of our lives and see that—financially, spiritually, and in every other way—the Gospel truly is Good News. And that God is faithful to his promises.

The Law of Sowing and Reaping

How do you position yourself to receive God's financial blessings and protection?

As I've already mentioned, you find out what God said about them in the Bible. You take the promises of His Word and plant them in your heart so they can grow up and produce a harvest.

You might not have thought of your Bible as a sack full of abundant life-producing seed, but according to Jesus that's what it is. It's not only a book of spiritual information, instructions, and encouragement. It's not just fuel for daily devotions or fodder for pastors' sermons. It's spiritual seed that contains the very Life of God Himself. It has the power to reproduce that Life—with all its blessings—in anyone who will plant and nurture it in the soil of their heart.

In Mark 4, Jesus explained this in parable form. He said:

Listen! Behold, a sower went out to sow. And it happened, as he sowed, that some seed fell by the wayside; and the birds of the air came and devoured it. Some fell on stony ground, where it did not have much earth; and immediately it sprang up because it had no depth of earth. But when the sun was up it was scorched, and because it had no root it withered away. And some seed fell among thorns; and the thorns grew up and choked it, and it yielded no crop. But other seed fell on good ground and yielded a crop that sprang up, increased and produced: some thirtyfold, some sixty, and some a hundred…He who has ears to hear, let him hear![111]

If Jesus had concluded His teaching there, most of us today would be like the original crowd who heard it. They left after the parable portion of the message and went home scratching their heads in confusion. They had no idea what Jesus was talking about.

Neither did the 12 disciples, at first. They were initially as clueless as everybody else, so after the crowd left, the disciples asked Jesus what the parable meant.

Kingdom Principles in Parables

Jesus' response was revealing. "You don't understand this parable?" He said. "How will you understand all the parables?"

In other words, Jesus regarded this teaching as the granddaddy of them all. It's the foundation that underlies every aspect of a successful and satisfying Christian life. To be productive in the Kingdom of God, we must be able to understand and implement the process of planting the Word and getting a harvest. Jesus didn't leave us in the dark about it. Explaining exactly what His parable meant, He said:

The sower sows the word. And these are the ones by the wayside where the word is sown. When they hear, Satan comes immediately and takes away the word that was sown in their hearts. These likewise are the ones sown on stony ground who, when they hear the word, immediately receive it with gladness; and they have no root in themselves, and so endure only for a time. Afterward, when tribulation or persecution arises for the word's sake, immediately they stumble. Now these are the ones sown among thorns; they are the ones who hear the word, and the cares of this world, the deceitfulness of riches, and the desires for other things entering in choke the word, and it becomes unfruitful. But these are the ones sown on good ground, those who hear the word, accept it, and bear fruit: some thirtyfold, some sixty, and some a hundred.[112]

Kingdom Wealth

The Word is the incorruptible seed that brings forth God's blessings and promises in our lives. It contains the revelation of our supernatural Covenant. That Covenant brought us and God together and gave us access to His wealth and influence. We had nothing to offer God, but He had everything to offer us, so He ratified His Covenant with us in the blood of Jesus. He took our weakness and lack and bestowed on us His strength and riches.

His riches don't just fall on us automatically, however, like apples off a tree. Even though they're ours in Jesus, we must provide the avenues for God to get them to us. We must open the door to His provision and miracles through our obedience, our faith and our faithfulness.

One key to doing this is understanding how much God loves us. The more we understand how much He cares and thinks about us, the easier it becomes for us to be obedient and stand in faith on His Word. That's why I like Psalm 115. It tells us how God thinks, by saying:

> The Lord has been mindful of us; He will bless us; He will bless the house of Israel; He will bless the house of Aaron. He will bless those who fear the Lord, Both small and great. May the Lord give you increase more and more, You and your children. May you be blessed by the Lord, Who made heaven and earth. The heaven,

even the heavens, are the Lord's; but the earth He has given to the children of men. [113]

Imagine it! God's thoughts are fixed on us! He remembers us day and night. He hasn't forgotten us or the things we're facing. He's constantly looking for ways to bring His best and His increase into our lives.

He's always done that for His Covenant people. He's always sought to bless them. Blessing is central to His heart for mankind. It's intrinsic to His nature. He's a Giver and a Blesser. That's exactly what He said when He established His covenant with Abram:

> The Lord…said to Abram: "Get out of your country, from your family and from your father's house, to a land that I will show you. I will make you a great nation; I will bless you and make your name great; and you shall be a blessing. I will bless those who bless you, and I will curse him who curses you; and in you all the families of the earth shall be blessed."[114]

The Amplified Classic Bible says it this way: "I will make of you a great nation, and I will bless you with abundant increase of favors."

God considered it a priority for His blessings and increase to be brought to mankind, and He chose Abram to bless first. Abram's only part was to believe and obey.

Not Enough Room

As Abram obeyed God, not only did his possessions increase, his nephew Lot's did too. Their flocks and herds multiplied to the point where they overwhelmed the land. Genesis 13:6 explains, "Now the land was not able to support them, that they might dwell together, for their possessions were so great that they could not dwell together."[115] In order to continue increasing, Abram and Lot had to separate and go different ways.

Abram walked in the kind of faith that is a model to all generations—the faith that pleased God. He was fully persuaded that his Covenant with God would bring Him increase. He expected God to bless him financially and that's exactly what happened, all the days of his life. He is called the father of faith.

In Genesis 17, God spoke to Abram again about His Covenant, changed his name from Abram to Abraham, and declared that He would "multiply him exceedingly." Afterward, God continued to increase Abraham in land, cattle, descendants, and wealth, prospering him in all aspects of his life.

What God did for Abraham is a picture of what He intends to do for you today. He has commanded His blessing on you being Abraham's heir. Why? Because as Galatians 3:29 says, "If you are Christ's, then you are Abraham's seed, and heirs according to the promise."[116]

Heirs of the Blessing

It's a wonderful thing to be Abraham's heir. That's evident by looking at Isaac, Abraham's son. God blessed him just as He blessed Abraham. At one point when a severe famine struck the land where Isaac was living, God protected him. Reaffirming His Covenant with him:

> The Lord appeared to Isaac and said, "Do not go down to Egypt, but do as I tell you. Live here as a foreigner in this land, and I will be with you and bless you. I hereby confirm that I will give all these lands to you and your descendants, just as I solemnly promised Abraham, your father.[117]

A famine is much worse than a recession. Yet Isaac stayed there in that famine-stricken land, obeyed God, and planted crops by faith. What happened? While the rest of the nation suffered through the famine:

> When Isaac planted his crops that year, he harvested a hundred times more grain than he planted, for the LORD blessed him. He became a very rich man, and his wealth continued to grow. He acquired so many flocks of sheep and goats, herds of cattle, and servants that the Philistines became jealous of him. [118]

Think about that. God didn't just see to it that Isaac survived. He didn't provide him with just enough to get by. He blessed Isaac so much that he harvested *100 times* more grain than he planted.

Can God do the same for us as heirs of Abraham today?

Yes.

Is it His will to do it?

Yes.

Has He promised it in His Covenant?

Yes.

Yet many in the Body of Christ haven't believed for that kind of abundance. They've struggled with the idea that God wants to increase them materially and work financial miracles in their lives. They've drawn back because they're afraid of becoming materialistic.

A couple of decades ago, the Lord gave Dennis this definition of materialism: *to endeavor to satisfy an emotional or spiritual need with a physical thing.* That's something no true believer wants to do. But it shouldn't make us shrink back from prosperity. Material increase is fine, if *we possess* the things, and don't allow them to *possess us.*

God made that clear by what He told King David. When David sinned and overstepped his position as king, God said to him, "I anointed you king over Israel, and I delivered you from the hand of Saul. I gave you your master's house...and gave you the house of Israel and Judah. *And if that had been too little, I also would have given you much more!*"[119]

Notice, God didn't rebuke David by telling him he possessed too much. He said He would have given David even more if he'd just asked. David had sinned, but it was not the wealth or power that was the problem. It was lust and covetousness.

The Miracle of Abundance

As New Testament believers, the power of sin has been broken over us through the blood of Jesus. So we don't have to fall prey to covetousness like David did. We can live upright before God, keep Him first place in our lives, and enjoy the blessing of financial abundance. We can safely receive the riches of our inheritance in Christ, and that's exactly what God wants us to do.

Abundance was so important to God that the first miracle Jesus performed in the Gospels was a miracle of abundance. During a wedding feast in Cana, the host ran out of wine to serve his guests. Jesus' mother told Him about the problem and then said to the servants, "Do whatever he tells you."

Jesus told the servants, "Fill the jars with water." When the jars had been filled to the brim, he said, "Now dip some out, and take it to the master of ceremonies." So they followed his instructions. When the master of ceremonies tasted the water that was now wine, not knowing where it had come from (though, of course, the servants knew), he called the bridegroom over. "A host always serves the best wine first," he said. "Then, when everyone has had a lot to drink, he brings out the less expensive wines. But you have kept the best until now!" This miraculous sign at Cana in Galilee was the first time Jesus revealed his glory.[120]

Isn't it amazing that's the way Jesus first revealed His glory? He didn't do it through a miracle of healing. He didn't do it by delivering someone from demonic power. He did it by miraculously supplying abundance and increase.

That is significant! Because Jesus did what He saw His Father do, it assures us that under the New Covenant, as under the Old, financial blessing and increase are included in His plan for His people.

To walk in that plan though, you must activate it in your life by believing and receiving God's promises. You must believe what God says about blessing you, just as Abraham believed the first words of blessing God spoke to him in Genesis.

Additionally, Deuteronomy 8:18 says, "The Lord your God...it is He who gives you power to get wealth, that He may establish His covenant which He swore to your fathers, as it is this day."[121] So never shrink back from or apologize for believing He will increase you. His financial blessings turns you into a testimony. They demonstrate to the world the power of God and His Covenant. They enable you to help finance the preaching of the Gospel so that God's Covenant can be established in lives all over the world.

This is God's promise to you: He gives you the power to get wealth. Even in times of economic crisis, recession, famine, or whatever, you can trust Him to not only protect you but increase you as well. He will shut you up in the Ark of His protection, and even though in the world the floods may come, and the storms may rage, you will be blessed!

MOLECULAR MIRACLE

R ain pounded our car as Dennis drove through rush hour traffic after visiting a friend in the hospital. Looking over at Dennis as we talked, I could see through the driver's side window beside him the huge grass median separating us from oncoming traffic. On our right, a white car sped alongside us, and behind it a semi blew spray onto the highway.

Suddenly, across the median, I saw a car hydroplane out of control. It hit the grass median going 60 or 70 miles per hour and headed straight for us.

"Look out!" I yelled.

The car crossing the median toward us never slowed. We were hemmed in. We couldn't swerve right because the white car was beside us in that lane. We couldn't slow down because of the semi was behind the white car. Traffic moved fast behind us.

As the car barreled toward us, I heard a cacophony of noise as inch-thick mud from the median splattered across our entire windshield. We couldn't see anything out of the windshield through the dense mud. But we did see the car out of the driver's side window just feet away, heading directly toward us. Dennis jerked our car to the right lane, and then off the road and stopped. We sat there, hearts racing, and looked around. How had the car with the maniac driver missed us? How had we gotten across the right lane without hitting the white car? Everything seemed surreal.

When we looked for the out of control car, it had come to a stop at the top of an exit ramp on our right. It had cut across both lanes of traffic behind us, missing the semi and other traffic, up an embankment and came to rest at the top of the elevated exit ramp.

"What happened to the white car next to us?" I asked. It seemed to have vanished before our eyes.

"We just experienced a molecular miracle," Dennis said. The white car was nowhere in sight.

Trusting God

Some misguided people think that God is out of the miracle business. Nothing could be farther from the truth. Miracles are still happening today and all it takes to experience them is to trust God's Word as your final authority. To begin a journey into a life of faith by trusting Him with the smallest of issues and to keep progressing until trusting Him with everything becomes as natural and automatic to you as breathing.

Such trust is available to all but like a muscle it must be developed. It must be exercised so that you can live your whole life doing what God said in Proverbs 3:5-6: "Trust in the Lord with all your heart; and do not depend on your own understanding. Seek His will in all you do, He will direct your paths."

That's how the Apostle Paul lived his life. It's also how he encouraged Timothy, his son in the Lord, to live. Although both men faced great danger as preachers of the Gospel, Paul told Timothy to have faith in God in every situation. Setting the example himself he wrote to Timothy that even in the midst of trouble and persecution, "I know the one in whom I trust, and I am sure that he is able to guard what I have entrusted to him until the day of his return."[122]

What confidence! What boldness! Paul expressed amazing assurance in that statement, and he wasn't just speaking lofty words. He was speaking from personal experience.

Paul had encountered more calamity and disaster in his life than we can begin to imagine. He was shipwrecked three times, once having to spend a day and a half in the sea. He was beaten three times. He faced danger not only in the city, but also in the country. He was attacked by robbers, went without food and water, and suffered from exposure. But none of those disasters could persuade him that God lacked the ability and willingness to deliver him.

Nor could they shake his confidence in God's unconditional love for him. As he said in Romans 8:

> No, in all these things we are more than conquerors through him who loved us. For I am convinced that neither death nor life, neither angels nor demons, neither the present nor the future, nor any powers, neither height nor depth, nor anything else in all creation, will be able to separate us from the love of God that is in Christ Jesus our Lord.[123]

The world doesn't have this kind of trust and confidence in God, but Paul did and so can we. Those who have a personal relationship with the Lord and are well acquainted with His goodness know His love. They've experienced His power, mercy, and faithfulness. They've developed such faith in Him that they're confident He won't fail them. They're convinced that in every circumstance He is not only able, but also delights in caring for and protecting His children.

Hoping Against Hope

We see in the Bible that Abraham, like Paul, was also fully convinced of God's ability to keep him and work miracles on his behalf. He believed God's promise about giving him a son, even though when God made that promise, he was not only beyond the age of having children, his wife Sarah was barren.

The situation seemed impossible. But "hoping against hope" Abraham believed God would do what He said.[124] Abraham didn't even let the weakness of his aging body cause him to waver. Instead, he let it serve to help him grow stronger in faith. He knew that only Almighty God could accomplish the impossible feat of making him a father, so he set his sights on experiencing a miracle. As a result, at the ripe old age of 99, he got one. He and Sarah had a son and witnessed firsthand the fulfillment of God's promise.

How was Abraham able to look this impossible situation square in the face and remain unmoved? Romans 4:21 tells us: He was "fully persuaded that, what he [God] had promised, he was able also to perform."[125] Abraham was completely convinced that God would do what man believed impossible.

In the New Testament, we see that Mary, the mother of Jesus, believed the same thing. When the angel of the Lord brought her the news that she would conceive and bear a son even though she'd never known a man, she didn't say such a thing couldn't happen. She just asked the angel *how* it would occur. "And the angel answered and said to her, 'The Holy Spirit will come upon you, and the power of the Highest will overshadow you…For with God nothing will be impossible.'"[126]

The Bible is full of situations where God performed the impossible when someone simply applied their faith. It assures us time and again that even in the face of impossibility, disaster, and calamity, we can be fully persuaded that God will protect, rescue, and deliver us. It also makes clear, however, that impossibility isn't what moves God. Faith is what moves God into action.

Do You Believe?

You can see this clearly when you study Jesus' ministry. He encountered many impossible situations and when He did, faith was always the first thing He looked for. Faith is the key to miracles. That's why when two blind men asked Jesus to heal them, instead of praying for them, He asked them a question. "Do you believe I can make you see?"

They said, "Yes, Lord, we do." And in response Jesus said, "Because of your faith, it will happen."[127]

Another time, the disciples found themselves unable to help a boy who was vexed by a demon. When they asked Jesus why they failed, He said, "You don't have enough faith…I tell you the truth, if you had faith as small as a mustard seed, you could say to this mountain, 'Move from here to there,' and it would move. Nothing would be impossible."[128]

It was never a desperate need, but faith, that moved Jesus when He was on earth, and He's the same today. He won't intervene in our lives just because we need help. But when we put our faith in Him, He'll do the impossible for us. He'll move on our behalf and we won't be disappointed or ashamed.

Jude 1:24 says that Jesus "is able to keep you from stumbling…."[129] He is able, as Paul put it in Second Timothy 1:12, to keep, attend to, guard, and preserve, what you have committed to Him until that Day. For Him to do so though, you must commit the concerns of your life to Him and refuse to remove them from His care. That's why Peter instructed us to, "Give all your worries and cares to God, for he cares about you."[130]

What types of things must you commit to Him?

First, commit your life. Then your health, your finances, your marriage, your children, and your safety. Commit everything that concerns you. Then confidently expect Jesus to apply to you what He said in the Gospel of John.

There, praying for His disciples, Jesus said, "Holy Father, you have given me your name; now protect them by the power of your name…I'm not asking you to take them out of the world, but to keep them safe from the evil one."[131]

Prayers of Intercession

Jesus didn't just pray those powerful prayers of intercession for His first twelve disciples. He prayed them for you and me, and they all have to do with keeping and guarding us against harm—protected and safe, right up to the end.

What's more, Jesus is still praying those prayers for us. He didn't stop when He left the earth. As Hebrews 7:25 explains, "He is able to save completely those who come to God through him, because he always lives to intercede for them."[132]

Think of it! Right now, Jesus is praying for you to be kept and guarded from evil by His resurrection power. Today, Jesus, who "gave himself for our sins, that he might deliver us from this present evil world" is interceding for you in Heaven at the right hand of God.[133]

In the Old Testament, Jabez prayed for God to keep and guard him from harm, and God answered him miraculously. "Jabez called on the God of Israel, saying, 'Oh, that you would bless me and extend my lands! Please be with me in all that I do, and keep me from all trouble and pain.' And God granted his request."[134]

How much more will God grant your request as a New Testament believer when you ask in faith for protection from harm? Certainly, if He did it for Jabez, Timothy and Paul, you can be sure He will do it for you.

Remember what First John 5:18 says, "The God-begotten are also the God-protected. The Evil One can't lay a hand on them."[135]

PROTECTION FROM FALSE ACCUSATIONS

D ennis and I were saddened when one of our friends from California phoned to say that his marriage was in trouble. His wife couldn't leave work at the time, but he flew to Texas and stayed with us for marriage counseling.

In the weeks our friend Robby[136] stayed with us, he went to church with us and made friends in the congregation. We had no idea that while he was getting marriage counseling from us, he was telling our friends he was divorced—and dating a woman named Grace.

Assuming Robby was sincere about restoring his marriage, the following weekend we flew his wife, Rachel, out so they could be in counseling together. The following Sunday morning, Robby and Rachel held hands during the church service, which enraged Grace.

Grace *claimed* the Lord told her, "That woman is holding your husband's hand." Of course, that was not the Holy Spirit speaking! Robby was, in fact, holding hands with his wife, Rachel.

As soon as we discovered Robby was dating someone, we asked him to find somewhere else to stay. We advised him to stop dating, tell the truth and return to his wife.

He didn't do that. Before long, Grace became offended. At us! She told our friends we were trying to ruin her wedding.

Wedding? They were getting married?

When Rachel called us one day, we asked her if she and Robby were divorced.

They weren't.

As the situation evolved, Dennis and I were considered the enemies of true love. Rumors flew, and even our friends believed them. Accusations swirled behind our backs, but no one asked us for the truth. We didn't believe in breaking confidences we'd heard in marriage counseling, and we refused to slander anyone.

Dennis and I knew that God promised to vindicate His people. These are some of the verses we stood on:

- "No weapon that is formed against you will prosper; and every tongue that accuses you in judgment you will condemn. This is the heritage of the servants of the LORD, and their vindication is from Me," declares the LORD.[137]

- I cry out to God Most High, to God, who vindicates me. [138]

- God will always be proven faithful and true to his word, while people are proven to be liars. This will fulfill what was written in the Scriptures: Your words will always be vindicated and you will rise victorious when you are being tried by your critics![139]

Standing on those promises, Dennis and I prayed, asking God to vindicate us. Then, keeping our mouths shut, we went about our business. A decade later, the truth about the situation came to light. At separate times, each of our critics apologized to us for siding against us without knowing the truth.

We kept our hearts clean and our mouths shut, and God vindicated us.

Protection from Slander

None of us is immune to the slander of an enemy or the betrayal of a friend. Even scriptural heroes like King David experienced it. The Bible says he was a man after God's own heart, yet he was lied about and plotted against by those around him time and again. How did he deal with it? He took it to the Lord. He prayed, as he did here in Psalm 56:

They are always twisting what I say. All their thoughts are how to harm me. They meet together to perfect their plans; they hide beside the trail, listening for my steps, waiting to kill me. They expect to get away with it. Don't let them, Lord. In anger cast them to the ground. You have seen me tossing and turning through the night. You have collected all my tears and preserved them in your bottle! You have recorded every one in your book. The very day I call for help, the tide of battle turns. My enemies flee! This one thing I know: God is for me![140]

God is for me! Those are wonderful words. And we as believers can say them with the same confidence David did. We can trust God to protect us, as he did David, from every onslaught of the enemy—including false accusations. Such protection is vital because Satan constantly uses accusations to attack us. As Revelation 12:10 says, he is "the accuser of our brothers…who accuses them before our God day and night."

God caused the evil events, plots, and plans against David to come upon his conspirators. If we'll stand on His Covenant promises, He'll do the same for us.

Saul's Attempts to Kill David

In Psalm 141, we find David praying again for protection and vindication. This time, his prayer was provoked by the persecution he was suffering at the hands of King Saul. He came after David with an entire army, hunting him down like an animal and accusing him of treason. In response, David went to the Lord and made this request: "Keep me out of the traps they have set for me, from the snares of those who do wrong. Let the wicked fall into their own nets, but let me escape."[141]

Repeatedly, God answered that prayer and kept David safe from every plot.

On one occasion, God protected him by sending Jonathan to plead his case with Saul and orchestrate David's escape. On another occasion, when Saul sent assassins to murder David in his bed, God moved on David's wife, Michal—who was also Saul's daughter—to protect him. She tricked the assassins by putting a bogus figure in David's bed and covered it with blankets. Then she helped him escape through a window.

Going through such things wasn't easy for David, of course. Like anyone would, he felt hurt and disappointed by his countrymen's betrayal. But through it all, he remained confident in the Lord and continued to look to Him for deliverance and vindication. He prayed:

"As for the head of those who surround me, may the mischief of their lips cover them. May burning coals fall upon them; may they be cast into the fire, into deep pits from which they cannot rise. May a slanderer not be established in the earth; may evil hunt the violent man speedily." I know that the Lord will maintain the cause of the afflicted, and justice for the poor. Surely the righteous will give thanks to Your name; the upright will dwell in Your presence.[142]

David was convinced that although men lied about him, the Lord would uphold his cause. He knew that those who spread false accusations only brought mischief upon themselves. He was so confident of it that in Psalm 7 he made this bold statement:

> If I have betrayed a friend…then let the enemy capture me. Let them trample me into the ground and drag my honor in the dust…The wicked conceive evil; they are pregnant with trouble and give birth to lies. They dig a pit to trap others and then fall into it themselves. The trouble they make for others backfires on them.[143]

There was no doubt in David's mind that God was a just judge who would reward the righteous while the wicked received retribution.

Pregnant With Trouble

This is just how God's system of justice is set up to work! Those who speak lies and conceive mischief become pregnant with their own trouble. They give birth to their own destruction. They position themselves for supernatural retribution and their wicked plans return upon their own heads.

David understood this. He was so convinced God would vindicate him that he didn't even try to defend himself. As he said in Psalm 38:12-14, "…my enemies lay traps for me; they make plans to ruin me. They think up treacherous deeds all day long. But I am deaf to all their threats. I am silent before them as one who cannot speak. I choose to hear nothing, and I make no reply."

In other words, David's response to persecution paralleled what the Bible says about Jesus. He didn't open his mouth. While being insulted, He didn't retaliate. He left His case in the hands of God, who always judges fairly.[144] He refused to justify or defend himself.

Instead, David committed his cause to the Lord. He relied upon Him to bring justice, rather than mounting his own defense. He took no action against those who had wronged him and remained silent. He chose to trust God to silence his enemies and put them to shame.

As believers, we're to do the same. That's what we did in the situation with Robby. But when we attempt to defend ourselves, we take God's work out of His hands. We forfeit the benefit of His Covenant promise to us.

The Worst Betrayal

The malice, hypocrisy, and insincerity that accompany disloyalty and false accusations are always hurtful. But when they come at you through family or friends, as they did in King David's life when his son, Absalom, betrayed him, it's especially painful and surprising.

David never suspected his own son would attempt to overthrow his throne. Yet that's exactly what Absalom did. He positioned himself at the city gate and began intercepting those seeking the king's counsel. He validated each person's cause and then told them the king was not available to help them. He manipulated them into siding with him by saying, "I wish I were the judge. Then everyone could bring their cases to me for judgment, and I would give them justice."[145]

What did David do when he found out about Absalom's treasonous plot to steal his throne? As always, rather than retaliating, he poured his heart out to the Lord. In his distress, he wrote Psalm 62:4. It says, "They plan to topple me from my high position. They delight in telling lies about me. They praise me to my face but curse me in their hearts."

Have you experienced that type of disloyalty—someone smiling to your face while cursing you behind your back? We all have. Did you respond like David? He turned to God as his only hope, waiting for His vindication. He put his trust in the Lord alone as his rock and salvation. Declaring his utter confidence in God's power to deliver him, he said boldly, "I shall not be shaken."

Talk about a dark time in his life. In that situation, even Ahithophel, David's most trusted advisor and friend betrayed him. Instead of staying loyal, he helped Absalom lead the revolt against David.

Ahithophel's defection was a severe blow to David. Speaking of it, in Psalm 55 David said, "It is not an enemy who taunts me—I could bear that. It is not my foes who so arrogantly insult me—I could have hidden from them. Instead, it is you—my equal, my companion and close friend…His words are as smooth as butter, but in his heart is war. His words are as soothing as lotion, but underneath are daggers!"[146]

Up until that time, Ahithophel's advice had been regarded in royal circles as wisdom from God. But when he betrayed David, God turned the tables on him. He caused Absalom to reject Ahithophel's counsel, and in his humiliation, Ahithophel killed himself. [147]

It was a sad ending for a once well-regarded man. But he brought it on himself. He put himself on the wrong side of God's Covenant of protection. As close as he'd been to David, he should have known that those who seek the ruin of God's people are arranging ruin for themselves. He should have remembered that, as Psalm 64:8-9 says, "Their own words will be turned against them, destroying them…Then everyone will stand in awe, proclaiming the mighty acts of God, realizing all the amazing things he does."

Haman's Plot

One of my favorite accounts of deliverance from false accusation is found in the book of Esther. It tells about a time in Jewish history when the Jews were living in Persia, and one of their own young women, Esther, became queen. After her coronation, her uncle Mordecai refused to bow down to the King's foremost official, who was a man named Haman.

Enraged by Mordecai's defiance, Haman decided to avenge himself not only by killing Mordecai but all the Jews in the country as well. He went to the king and said:

> There is a certain race of people scattered through all the provinces of your empire. Their laws are different from those of any other people, and they refuse to obey even the laws of the king. So it is not in the king's interest to let them live. If it please the king, issue a decree that they be destroyed, and I will give 10,000 large sacks of silver to the government administrators to be deposited in the royal treasury. The king agreed, confirming his decision by removing his signet ring from his finger and giving it to Haman son of Hammedatha the Agagite, the enemy of the Jews. The king said, "The money and the people are both yours to do with as you see fit."[148]

When news of Haman's plot reached Queen Esther, she realized the fate of Mordecai and her people rested in her hands. If they were to survive, she would have to go to the king and intervene for them. Even as queen, to approach the king without an invitation meant certain death, unless he extended his scepter, then she would live. So, she called a three day fast among all the Jews and then went to see the king.

When Esther approached the king, he was pleased with her and extended his scepter. Then he asked, "What is your desire?" Esther invited both the king and Haman to a banquet that evening. At the banquet, the king asked Esther, "Now, what is it you want?"[149] Once again, she asked that both the king and Haman would dine with her the following evening.

The night before the second banquet, the king couldn't sleep. Getting up, he asked that the record of his reign be read to him. As he listened, he found out it had been recorded in the book that Mordecai had stopped an assassination plot against him. Yet, nothing had been done to honor him.

The Tide Turned

The next morning, King Xerxes asked Haman what should be done for the man who pleased the king. Haman wrongly assumed the king wanted to honor *him*, so he said, "Have them bring a royal robe the king has worn and a horse the king has ridden, one with a royal crest placed on its head…Let them robe the man the king delights to honor, and lead him on the horse through the city streets, proclaiming before him, 'This is what is done for the man the king delights to honor!'" [150]

Imagine Haman's horror when the king ordered him to do those things for Mordecai. After leading Mordecai, dressed in the king's robe and riding his horse, through the streets, Haman attended the feast that night with Queen Esther. That evening, she revealed to the king Haman's plot to have her and her people killed. Haman was hung on the gallows he'd built for Mordecai.

What amazing vindication!

Not only for Mordecai, but for God's people as well. We're told in Esther 9:1, "On this day the enemies of the Jews had hoped to overpower them, but now the tables were turned and the Jews got the upper hand over those who hated them."[151]

Notice how God reversed the course of events so that the evil intended for His people came upon those who plotted it. Although the enemies of God's people think they are wiser than God, First Corinthians 3:19 says, "For the wisdom of this world is foolishness to God. As the Scriptures say, 'He traps the wise in their own cleverness.'" God sees the plots of the wicked while they're still in the planning stage and thwarts them before they come to fruition. But that doesn't happen automatically, it only happens for those who believe for His supernatural protection.

No weapon can prove strong enough to do harm to God's children. The Apostle Paul testified to the strength of God's weapons saying, "For the weapons of our warfare are not carnal but mighty in God for pulling down strongholds."[152]

You have a Covenant with God that promises you every false accusation spoken against you will either miss its mark or return to the one who made it. Those who speak against you are preparing weapons for themselves. When words rise against you, as they did the Jews, they'll be proven wrong.

Vindication is your heritage, just as it was for Dennis and me. Claim that powerful promise as your own!

TERROR AT HOME

Worldwide terrorism has become part of the fabric of life in these perilous times. But countless thousands of people—adults and children—live with terror at home. I know this to be true, because I was one of them.

You see, I was suicidal at the age of nine.

One of four children, we lived in a middle-class home in Southern California. Our house was nice enough, but that's where normal ended.

My father was an alcoholic. My mother was a rage-aholic. Nine years of living in constant fear and abuse had taken a toll on my mental and emotional health. A constant diet of violence and beatings had taught me something.

I didn't want to live anymore.

The very thought of another nine years of what I'd already experienced felt unbearable. Yet that's what I'd have to endure to make it to my 18th birthday when I'd be old enough to escape. Sadly, the Roman Catholic services we attended on Easter and Christmas were in Latin, I had no idea what was said. If there was hope for me in God, I never knew it.

One thing Catholicism did teach though was that suicide was a mortal sin. It would land you in hell faster than a snake could strike. We all knew that. I had already lived in enough hell, I certainly didn't want to spend eternity there.

So, when my mother bought a new organ and learned a hymn from the music book that came with it, it gave me an idea. The hymn was called "It Is No Secret," and the lyrics said "with arms wide open He'll pardon you."

Thinking of the lyrics to that song, I slipped out of the house into the backyard. I sat cross-legged on the grass and threw my arms up toward God and prayed the most desperate and heartfelt prayer of my young life.

"God," I prayed, "please kill me."

If I felt rage from the constant beatings, that was nothing compared to the utter betrayal I felt toward God. No matter how many times I opened my arms wide to Him and prayed, He didn't take my life. I kept waiting to die, but it didn't happen.

Didn't He care? Was He uninterested in my despair?

To me, violence was a regular part of everyday life. One day as I walked along the sidewalk that ran alongside a cinder block fence leading from the back to the front yard, a bullet shot through the wall out of our house, whizzed past my head and drilled a hole into the cement wall. For some reason, I didn't give it a second thought.

I just kept walking.

The Danger of a Locked Door

Even though Dad was an alcoholic, he was the more stable parent. We all despised my mother. It was her rage that kept the violence boiling. I was in middle school when I came home one day and found the front door locked. Back then, nobody locked their doors. I knew something was very wrong.

I ran to the back door and slipped inside. In the living room, I saw my dad straddling my mother holding a gun to her temple. My eyes met Dad's and locked. Our thoughts were as clear as if they'd been spoken aloud.

How could we kill her and get away with it?

Silence hung like a shroud over the house as I thought about it.

We all wanted her out of our lives. That wasn't an issue. But what if something went wrong and Dad went to prison? What would happen to us? I couldn't imagine anything worse than our situation, but what if there *was* something worse?

I heaved a deep sigh. "Do you want me to call an ambulance and tell them that Mom had a nervous breakdown?"

Dad dropped his head and sighed too. "Yeah."

Even at that age, I knew that Dad's presence was the only governor that kept my simmering rage in check.

I seldom asked friends over because I didn't want anyone to see what went on behind closed doors. However, when I was 15, my best friend Nikki came to visit. My parents were taking us out to eat, and my friend and I went to my bedroom to get ready.

One of the many things my mother hated was my hair. It was straight as a nun's wimple and parted down the middle. Mom took the brush out of my hand and scraped it across my head to try to get my hair to go another way.

It fell back into the middle part.

She slapped me across the face.

Then she brushed it again—and slapped me.

Again. Again. Again.

This went on for the better part of half an hour, by which time I was crying hysterically.

When we arrived at the café, I was still sort of hiccupping and sobbing. "If you don't shut up right now," Dad warned, "I'm going to give you something to cry about."

Nobody within the sound of his voice doubted that he meant every word.

Nikki had never seen this side of my family. She had been so outraged at what she'd witnessed that she collected money from friends and suggested we run away together the next night. Although our foolish plan to run away failed, Nikki's commitment to help me escape showed more compassion than I'd ever experienced.

Just when I thought things couldn't get any worse, they did. When I was 16, Dad died of cancer. My rage spun out of control. I stood over my mother and said, "For 16 years you've tormented me. Now the tide has turned." I grabbed her by the throat with every intention of choking her to death.

My brother pulled me from her. Now I'm thankful he wouldn't let me do it.

A Spirit of Fear

The fear that had been incubated in my life since conception, mushroomed into a sinister cloud I couldn't escape. I had no idea back then that fear wasn't just a feeling, or that the Bible called it a *spirit of fear*. All I knew was that I trusted no one. I was terrified that someone was out to get me. That's when I started sleeping with a hand ax under my pillow.

Three years later I was born again, but the anger I felt toward my mother still had a grip on me. I knew it was wrong to harbor these feelings, but I didn't know how to get rid of them. It didn't begin to budge until one day when I was 23, I was driving to work, and I heard a voice: *"Say that you love your mother."*

"I *hate* my mother!" I growled.

At the time I didn't know it was the Holy Spirit speaking to me. Looking back now, it's hilarious to think that I'd conquered the need to sleep with a hand ax but hearing voices didn't strike me as crazy.

The conversation repeated itself weekly for months. God wouldn't give up, and I refused to give in. One day I snarled, "Okay! I'll say it! I love my mother! But we both know I really hate her!"

The voice continued for the next six months, *"Say that you love your mother."*

My calloused response became routine, "Okay, I love my mother!"

After months of saying those words, something drastically changed. It's as though a light turned on in my soul. The compassion of God for my mother welled up in me, and I wept for her. I saw Mom in an entirely new light. I saw into the struggle she had lived with. God gave me the understanding that she couldn't give what she didn't have. She'd been abused, so she abused.

I was dramatically changed. Without knowing what had happened back then, God was paving the path for my future by freeing me from my past. The words I spoke shattered the wall that anger had built. I thought the wall was protecting me, but it had actually imprisoned me.

It would be years before I'd realized the Holy Spirit had used my own words to change my heart. Just like it promises in Mark 11:23, that we can have what we say. All I knew at the time was when I repeatedly said that I loved my mother—I *did*.

Forgiving her released the chains that the enemy had used to hold me in bondage for years. My mother wasn't an easy person to love, but I did love her. Years later, I considered it a privilege to take care of her for the last three years of her life.

Forgive to Be Forgiven

God knew (even if I didn't) that holding onto anger and unforgiveness would stop my faith from working—and faith is essential. Hebrews 11:6, tell us that "without faith it is impossible to please Him" and in Galatians 5:6 that "faith worketh by love." [153]

Much later the Lord spoke this to me: "Forgiveness is the language of Heaven." Well, of course! Forgiveness is the whole point of what Jesus did for us on Calvary. He forgave us *everything*. The only thing that can stop Him from forgiving now is if we don't forgive others.

Jesus made this clear in Mark 11:25-26. "Whenever you stand praying," He said, "if you have anything against anyone, forgive him, that your Father in heaven may also forgive you your trespasses. But if you do not forgive, neither will your Father in heaven forgive your trespasses."[154]

Ouch. No wonder the Lord spent six months getting me to forgive my mother! Clinging to offense is serious business. It will hinder our prayers and pull down our walls of protection. It will keep us from receiving God's forgiveness ourselves and even block the manifestation of God's healing power in our lives.

"But Vikki," you might say, "Is it really possible to live free from offense every day, no matter what's going on around us?"

Yes!

Psalm 119:165 says, "Great peace have they which love thy law: and *nothing shall offend them.*"[155] So, clearly such a life is possible.

It isn't exactly easy though—especially in our day. The closer we come to the end of the age, the more we have opportunities to become hurt and offended. Those stepped-up opportunities are part of the plan of our enemy and we play right into his hand when we take his bait.

He wants us to fall for them because wounded and offended people pose no threat to the kingdom of darkness. They're also not very useful to the Kingdom of God. Hurt people waste a great deal of otherwise productive time and energy struggling to make sense of wrong situations.

One person might spend his time asking God why a certain situation happened. Someone else might spin his wheels as he justifies his reasons for acting the way he did. Still another might replay the events in a vicious mental cycle, only to end up more hurt and angrier than before.

People's reactions to offensive situations differ. But in every case, one fact remains the same: hurt and anger go hand-in-glove.

Mom Wasn't the Enemy

How do we deal with hurt and anger without getting offended?

We remember that although people do hurt us sometimes, they're not our real enemies. The devil and his evil forces are our true adversaries. As Ephesians 6:12 says, "For we are not fighting against flesh-and-blood enemies, but against the evil rulers and authorities of the unseen world, against mighty powers in this dark world, and against evil spirits in the heavenly places."

When people hurt or attack us, whether they realize it or not, they're being used as pawns of the enemy to entrap us. Entrapment is the devil's whole purpose behind offense. The original Greek word for offense, which is *skandalon,* literally means *a snare; to trip up; to entice to sin.* Another word that can be used for it is *trap-stick.*

What exactly is a trap-stick?

According to *Thayer's Greek Lexicon*, it's "the movable stick or tricker ('trigger') of a trap; snare; any impediment placed in the way and causing one to stumble or fall." I envision it as a stick that props up a cage that's designed to trap an animal. When the animal bumps the stick, the cage falls around the animal and becomes its prison.

Vine's Expository Dictionary further defines *skandalon* as "the name of the part of a trap to which the bait is attached, hence, the trap or snare itself...." *Vine's* adds that skandalon is "...anything that arouses prejudice, or becomes a hindrance to others, or causes them to fall by the way."

Jesus considered the bait of offense to be so dangerous to us as believers He made this shocking allegorical statement: "If your right eye causes you to sin, pluck it out and cast it from you; for it is more profitable for you that one of your members perish, than for your whole body to be cast into hell."[156]

When I look back over my life, my entire childhood was baited with traps the enemy set to destroy me. If I didn't die from the violence, the enemy hoped to pressure me until I committed suicide. He almost succeeded. He tried to torment me into killing myself. If neither of those things worked, his strategy was to ensnare me with such offences and bitterness that I would never be free.

Offense Comes with Purpose

One way hurt and offense robs us as believers of our freedom is it keeps us focused on ourselves. It serves the demonic purpose of distracting us from that which is most important in life—the freedom God has provided.

That's what happened to Jesus' friend, Martha. When her sister Mary chose to sit and listen to Jesus instead of help with dinner, Martha got offended and let her distractedness and preoccupation steal from her the opportunity to listen to Jesus' teaching herself. When Martha accused Jesus of not caring about her situation, He corrected her, saying: "… Martha, dear Martha, you're fussing far too much and getting yourself worked up over nothing. One thing only is essential, and Mary has chosen it—it's the main course, and won't be taken from her."[157]

As Martha's case demonstrates, when we become distracted and worked up over a problem, the enemy has achieved his purpose: Our focus is diverted from the Word of God and we're left to solve our problems ourselves with only our limited understanding and our natural reasoning. That's tragic! Only God's Word can deliver us from every problem—whether self-induced or provoked by an outsider. So, without the Word we have no way of escape.

The Apostle Paul confirmed this. After facing many hopeless situations, he concluded that relying on himself to solve his problems was equivalent to a death sentence. Even when

he was literally about to die for his faith, Paul's utter depen-
dence was so profound that he not only attributed his survival
to his reliance on God alone, he penned this promise: "He has
delivered us from such a deadly peril, and he will deliver us
again. On him we have set our hope that he will continue to
deliver us."[158]

Offense Hinders the Anointing

Another way offense and hurt robs us as believers is by
hindering the flow of the anointing of God. Why does the
enemy want the anointing hindered? It overturns his ugly
works. It releases God's supernatural power to accomplish His
will in us and through us.

The prophet Isaiah said, "It shall come to pass...that [the
enemy's] burden shall be taken away from off thy shoulder,
and his yoke from off thy neck, and the yoke shall be destroyed
because of the anointing."[159] That means the anointing has the
power to both remove and destroy the burdens the enemy tries
to use to overload us. It also means that without the anointing,
we'll succumb to those heavy burdens.

Even though the anointing is available to us in Christ, if
we can't apply it by faith because we're offended, we won't live
in its benefits. Its burden-removing, yoke-destroying ability
will remain for us only *potential* power.

That's what happened when Jesus ministered in Nazareth.
Even though it was His hometown and He was as anointed

with the Holy Spirit and power in Nazareth just as He was in other places, the people there didn't receive much from Him. They didn't benefit from the anointing that was on Him because they'd taken offense.

What caused them to take offense? *Familiarity.* They got mad at Jesus because they'd known Him since He was a child and they couldn't see how He could be anointed by God.

"Where did he get all this wisdom and the power to perform such miracles?" Then they scoffed, "He's just the carpenter, the son of Mary and brother of James, Joseph, Judas, and Simon. And his sisters live right here among us."[160]

Their attitude resulted in their refusing to believe in Him and restricted their ability to receive the anointing that was on Him. Because they refused to accept the Person through whom God had chosen to work, Jesus "…couldn't do any mighty miracles among them except to place his hands on a few sick people and heal them."[161]

Sometimes we as believers today find ourselves in this situation with our own relatives and friends. We want to minister to them and pray for them, but they won't believe we have anything to give them. Like the people in Jesus' hometown who chose not to believe that God would use a Person with whom they were so familiar, those who are familiar with us often make the same unfortunate choice.

In the Old Testament, David encountered a similar attitude in his brothers just before his battle against Goliath.

Every warrior in Israel had cowered under Goliath's threatening words and massive size, so when David first inquired about him, David's older brother, Eliab, became angry. "What are you doing around here anyway?" he demanded. "What about those few sheep you're supposed to be taking care of? I know about your pride and deceit. You just want to see the battle!"[162]

Eliab was especially bitter toward David because as Jesse's firstborn son, Eliab typically would have been chosen as the one to be anointed as king. But God had refused Eliab, along with his six younger brothers. Instead God had instructed the prophet Samuel to anoint David, Jesse's youngest son, to be king of Israel.

Apparently, Eliab remained so deeply offended toward David that he constantly criticized him. So, in response to Eliab's sarcastic comments about the situation with Goliath, David replied, "What have I done now? I was only asking a question!"[163]

Despite his brothers' fault-finding though, David never allowed their hurtful words to enter his heart. Instead, just as he protected his sheep from all predators, he protected his heart and the anointing of God which had always caused him to succeed. So when the time came to face Goliath, David was ready.

When Goliath hurled his insults at the God of Israel, a righteous indignation arose in David and he declared with boldness, "The Lord who rescued me from the claws of the lion and the bear will save me from this Philistine!"[164]   He brought the power of God's anointing into manifestation to win the day.

Jesus Set the Example

Jesus was the greatest example of someone who refused to take offense. No matter how people came against Him, no matter what wrong choices they made, He never allowed anything to hurt, embitter, or distract Him. He never got his attention on how people responded to His ministry.

Jesus knew that the choices people made were not His responsibility. His responsibility was to fully please and obey God. So He remained focused on what God had called Him to do.

You can see this in Matthew 16. There, Jesus tried to explain to the disciples the suffering He would have to endure to fulfill God's plan of redemption, and Peter reacted badly. He actually rebuked Jesus. Taking Jesus aside, Peter corrected Him and said, "Heaven forbid, sir," he said. "This is not going to happen to you!"[165]

Jesus responded by saying, "Get away from me, Satan! You are a dangerous trap to me. You are thinking merely from a human point of view, and not from God's."[166]

The phrase 'dangerous trap' that Jesus used comes from that same Greek word *skandalon*, that means *offense*. Peter didn't realize that Satan was using him to tempt Jesus into focusing on something other than the will of God. But Jesus recognized Peter's comment for what it was: *a dangerous trap.* He was quick to recognize and to resist Satan's bait.

Jesus was always that way. He lived His entire life on earth without becoming ensnared in offense. How did He do it? *He kept His heart guarded with the Word of God.*

If we want to avoid Satan's traps in our own lives, we must do the same. We must heed Solomon's warning: "Above all else, guard your heart, for it affects everything you do."[167] Other versions of that verse identify the heart as *the wellspring from which life flows.*

Many people open their hearts carelessly. They expect others to treat them with the same kindness and honesty they give out. Though that would be nice, it's not how the world operates. People who open their unguarded hearts to everyone may wind up getting their hearts crushed.

When your heart is left unguarded—open to every assault that comes your way—you're certain to be a vulnerable target for the enemy. So, take responsibility and protect your wellspring of life. Guard your heart diligently from those who would wound it.

Is it possible to guard my heart from the hurtful actions of others without becoming hardhearted? you might wonder.

Yes—but only as you choose to keep God's Word before your eyes and in your heart. Only as you heed what He says in Proverbs 4:21: "Don't lose sight of my words. Let them penetrate deep within your heart."

Psalm 119:165 promises those who love God's Word that "...nothing shall offend them or make them stumble." So, if we keep our eyes fixed on God's promises and love His Word above all else, no matter how much outward circumstances try to crowd in and dictate our emotions, we can live in great peace and nothing will trip us up.

God's Word will protect us from all the dangerous traps our enemy sets for us. It helps us recognize and resist Satan's bait when our relatives and friends say hurtful things to us. It prevents us from reacting in agitation or anger when others choose to live their lives their way instead of yielding to the Lord.

God has given every human being the right to choose how he or she will live. You're only responsible for the choices you make, not for the choices of others. So make the decision to recognize and resist offense, no matter what anyone says or does. Choose to keep your eyes fixed on the promise of God, regardless of what's going on around you. That way you'll become a candidate for all the benefits of God's blessings.

AVOIDING THE TRAPS

16

When I'm not praying in the rocking chair on my front porch, I like to take prayer walks. I've been prayer walking four miles for over 35 years. On one walk, the Lord led me to pray protection for some friends.

On my walk to the park, I crossed a four-lane street. Two lanes going east; two lanes going west. As I stepped off the curb, a car hit the median with such force that the wheel was broken completely off the axle.

The wheel soared through the air, landing behind me in the exact spot where I'd stood just seconds before. I looked back, shocked by the sight. I never saw it coming.

When we make a habit of speaking our covenant promises daily, God is on the scene protecting us even when we're unaware of the danger. His angels surround us. I'm confident my prayer for protection diverted that wheel so it didn't land on me.

There are booby traps laid for us by the enemy—and this was one of them. But I was literally walking in the secret place of the Most High, so I escaped the trap.

Jesus did that all the time when He was on earth. He constantly sidestepped the booby traps that Satan set for Him. When religious leaders ambushed Him with hostile questions designed to trip Him up, He dodged each one with greater finesse than a seasoned attorney. When a crowd got angry with Him one time over what He preached and led Him to the edge of a cliff with every intention of throwing Him over, He simply turned around and walked away. [168]

In every situation, Jesus remained in complete control.

How did He do it? What kept Him from being drawn into Satan's snares?

One of His secrets was this: He never allowed human opinion to affect Him. He said this Himself very plainly. Speaking to a group of powerful leaders, He said, "Your approval or disapproval means nothing to me...." [169]

Fear Disables

Proverbs 29:25 warns, "Fearing people is a dangerous trap...." *The Message* Bible says, "The fear of human opinion *disables*...."

If fear *dis*ables, then fearlessness *en*ables. It empowers us to operate in the wisdom of God and to trust Him.

This is the principle we see operating in Jesus' life. Human opinion didn't affect Him at all. How could He live free from human opinion? Because He always did what pleased the Father.[170] He lived fearlessly, trusted the Lord, and walked in safety. He remained mindful of the spiritual climate in every situation, so when He encountered opposition He didn't react in the flesh. Instead, He looked beyond human actions or opinions to identify their source.

He followed the fruit to the root.

Jesus understood that although *people* harassed and attacked Him, they were not the root of the problem. The root was Satan himself, and people's behaviors were just the fruit of his schemes. Jesus never retaliated when people attacked or insulted Him because He knew full well that His battle was against spiritual opponents. His conflict was not with people but with unseen powers of darkness.

Because He knew this, Jesus was able to sidestep every trap the enemy set for Him. And He intends for us to do the same—to realize that fighting people is a waste of time. If we want to avoid being affected by Satan's fruit—such as opposition, criticism, or personal attacks through other people—we must stop spending all our time trying to deal with problems at the human level and deal with the *root*.

Sidestep the Trap

If Jesus could do this, certainly we can. He had more problems to deal with than any of us ever will. His life wasn't trouble-free! He was despised and rejected, a man of sorrow and familiar with grief. [171]

He faced angry mobs, accusations from powerful leaders, insults, temptations, beatings, and crucifixion. He had to use God's wisdom to navigate dangerous, mine-infested waters and avoid the countless booby traps of the devil. Even traps set up through religious people.

Time and again, "the Pharisees met together to think of a way to trap Jesus into saying something for which they could accuse him."[172] Time and again, they acted as the devil's pawns and tried to get Him to say something wrong. Yet Jesus never defended Himself or got offended at them.

He just kept saying what God said and refused to say anything else. He kept His heart so free of offense and His mouth so full of God's Word that when His life was over, He could say, "The prince of this world…has no hold over me."[173]

Satan couldn't lay a finger on Jesus unless He said something that gave the devil access to His life. He couldn't ensnare Jesus at all unless he could get Him to say words that were contrary to God's truth. The same is true for believers.

Proverbs 18:21 says, "Death and life are in the power of the tongue."[174] Proverbs 6:2 says, "You are taken as in a net by the words of your mouth; the sayings of your lips have overcome you."[175] Jesus knew those verses. He understood the power of His words. So He made sure that everything that came out of His mouth agreed with God's Word and stayed out of Satan's net.

Fiery Darts

If we're to stay out of Satan's snare, we must understand the power of our words too. We must remember that every fiery dart Satan throws at us is designed to get us to say something that will give him access to our lives. That's the Satanic agenda behind all harassment against us and every hurtful deed done to us. The enemy's goal is to get hold of our tongue.

We don't have to let him do it though. Once we become aware of how important our words are, we can be more vigilant about them. We can pray as David did, "Set a guard over my mouth, Lord; keep watch over the door of my lips,"[176] and by the grace of God we can keep our mouth in line.

I'm not suggesting, of course, that when we do this Satan will stop putting pressure on us. I'm not saying he'll give up just because we've caught onto his tactics. On the contrary. He'll most likely re-double his efforts. He'll not only keep trying to trap us, he'll escalate his attacks.

That's what he did with Jesus. When the Pharisees' failed in their initial attempts to entrap Him, instead of sending them home the enemy continued to stir up their antagonism.

He kept goading them, "they grilled him with many hostile questions, trying to trap him into saying something they could use against him."[177]

They tried to trap Him about all kinds of different subjects. They pressed Him to give His opinion about divorce, taxes, the importance of keeping tradition, adultery, the most important commandment, and the way to get to Heaven. But Jesus never took the bait. He never got upset, gave His opinion, or engaged in their debate.

Instead He dashed the devil's hopes and thwarted his agenda. He resisted Satan's every attempt to get hold of His tongue and used Scripture to answer every question. Pointing His adversaries to God's Word. He continued to say, "It is written."

And He expects us to do the same.

It Is Written

One thing that can help us do that is learning the lesson Jesus taught in Matthew 16. After the Pharisees and Sadducees had pummeled Him with questions and accusations, Jesus said to His disciples, "Watch out!...Beware of the yeast of the Pharisees and Sadducees."[178]

His warning initially puzzled the disciples. They thought He was talking about natural bread and natural yeast. But Jesus quickly made it clear that He wasn't talking about food at all.

He was alerting them to one of Satan's methods of trapping people. He was comparing the enemy's strategies to yeast.

What does yeast do? According to the dictionary, it *agitates or causes fermentation; leaven (rising)*. It *causes a state of commotion, unrest, or boiling up.* That's exactly what Satan does! He uses people and situations to try to agitate, bring unrest, and commotion. He uses them to try to get us angry so we'll boil over and lose control.

Satan knows if he can get a rise out of us, we'll lose our cool. We'll step out of the realm of the Spirit into the realm of the flesh where he rules. Once we're there, we'll be vulnerable to him and he can entrap us.

Legally, entrapment refers to a situation where *a person is induced or persuaded to commit an act he had no previous intention of committing.* That's the situation the devil wants to get us into. He wants to trick us into yielding to the flesh and saying something foolish so that he can hang us with our own words.

One way he accomplishes this is by magnifying minor irritations. Like yeast, he goes to work and inflates them. He puffs up problems and negative situations, so they appear to us to be much bigger than they are.

Just think about the last time you lost your cool. What upset you may have been no big deal in the overall scheme of things. It might have been something as simple as a car cutting in front of you. Or the clerk at the grocery store being too slow.

When you get in the flesh, it only takes a small amount of yeast to get a big rise. So as the Apostle Paul wrote, "Walk in the Spirit, and you shall not fulfill the lust of the flesh."[179] Ask the Holy Spirit to help you recognize the devil's yeast before it has its agitating effect on you. Remember that you're in a conflict between kingdoms, watch out for the traps Satan is setting for you, and refuse to take the bait.

If you'll do that, the next time a situation arises that would push your button, you'll be ready to resist the temptation to get agitated. You'll be able to yield to the fruit of the spirit, such as longsuffering, patience, and gentleness. Then those petty irritants won't be able to agitate you the way they once did.

You'll be able to declare with confidence, "The devil has *no hold* on me."

FATAL ATTRACTION

The Washington DC office of Senate Majority Leader Tom Daschle bustled with activity on October 15, 2001. Phones rang, people rushed about to meetings and the mailman delivered stacks of mail. When an employee opened a letter from Trenton, New Jersey, a white, powdery substance fell out.

It was weapon's grade anthrax.

More than two dozen people in Daschle's office tested positive for the anthrax.

It wasn't the first time someone had used the postal system and an envelope to deliver a biological weapon. Seven days after the attacks on September 11, 2001, anonymous letters laced with anthrax spores began arriving at media companies and congressional offices.

The first person to contract the disease was Bob Stevens, a photo editor at American Media, Inc. Over the ensuing months, five people died and 17 others were infected. Among the victims was NBC News anchor Tom Brokaw's assistant, and the seven-month-old son of an ABC News reporter.

Anthrax is an acute infectious disease caused by bacterium Bacillus anthracis. It's spread through skin contact, ingestion and inhalation of the spores. Over the years, anthrax plagues have killed both humans and animals.

It emerged as a biological weapon in World War II.

What about anthrax? Can God protect us even from a plague like that? Absolutely. And He promised us in the Bible that He would do so. Addressing the issue very specifically in Psalm 91:5-6, He assured us that our Covenant with Him includes protection from every kind of attack the enemy can formulate. "You shall not be afraid of the terror by night," He said, "Nor of the arrow that flies by day, Nor of the pestilence that walks in darkness...."[180]

The word *pestilence* in that verse is translated from the Hebrew word *deber*. According to the dictionary, it refers not only to pestilence but to *plagues or murrain*. We don't commonly use the word *murrain* these days, but if you look it up, you'll find it refers to an infectious cattle disease such as anthrax.

God has us covered! He knew thousands of years ago that anthrax in the hands of wicked men could be a fatal weapon. Therefore, He provided us with protection against it in His Word.

When you put your faith in God's promise in Psalm 91, you don't have to fear any pestilence. You can live at peace, without dread of evil, confident that God has delivered you from anthrax, swine flu and every other plague.

Strong in the Face of Adversity

To have such confidence in our day and age is a great blessing because, as I've already mentioned, we're living in what the Bible calls "the last days." Second Timothy 3:1 says these days will be "perilous times of great stress and trouble [hard to deal with and hard to bear]."[181] They won't be impossible to bear though. Even at their worst, they'll just be hard.

There's a significant difference between impossible and hard. We can deal with and overcome hard things. It just takes increased strength and determination. Where do we get that strength?

From God's Word.

It has the power to carry us through any situation. To lift us up when circumstances try to get us down. It enables us to remain calm no matter what's going on around us and say like the psalmist did, "As pressure and stress bear down on me, I find joy in your commands."[182]

We don't have to be pathetic, weak people who let these troubled times overcome us. We can tap into God's supernatural strength by filling our hearts with the Scriptures. As Jesus said, "These things I have spoken to you, that in Me you may have peace. In the world you will have tribulation; but be of good cheer, I have overcome the world."[183]

It sounds simple, I know, but it's the truth: A consistent, daily time of prayer and meditation in God's Word can give you all the power you need to be strong in times of adversity. Neglecting the Word, on the other hand, will leave you lacking. If you don't spend time in the Word in advance, before trouble comes, you'll be like the person Proverbs 24:10 describes. You'll "faint in the day of adversity, [because] your strength is small." [184]

The *Living Bible* says, "You are a poor specimen if you can't stand the pressure of adversity." Ouch! I don't ever want to be thought of as a poor specimen, do you? A poor specimen is a person who is fainthearted. It's a Christian who worries, for example, at the very thought of trouble. Instead of meditating on the answers found in the promises of God, a worrier meditates on *what if....*

What if I get on an airplane that is highjacked?

What if I catch some fatal disease?

What if a student brings a gun to my child's school and begins shooting students?

Worrying about such things is a sign that your spiritual strength is small or limited. But here's the good news: You don't have to stay in that weakened condition.

Any time you make the decision to do so, you can tap into the supernatural power of God. You can build your spiritual muscles by feasting on a steady diet of His Word. As Isaiah 40:29 promises, "He gives power to the weak and strength to the powerless." And when you're walking in His power you can defeat anything that comes against you or your family.

Control Your Thoughts

To walk in God's power though, you must get rid of fear because fear and faith are opposing spiritual forces. One counteracts the other. Trying to operate in them both at the same time is like trying to get both sweet water and bitter water to come out of the same fountain—and as James said in the New Testament, that's impossible.

Just as faith activates the forces of the kingdom of God, fear activates the forces of the kingdom of darkness. It attracts the very thing it focuses upon. Remember what happened to Job? He literally drew calamity to himself by yielding to fear. He said it himself: "What I always feared has happened to me. What I dreaded has come true." [185]

Talk about fatal attraction! The *Adam Clarke Commentary* renders Job's statement this way: "The fear that I feared. While I was in prosperity, I thought adversity might come, and I had a dread of it. I feared the loss of my family and my property; and both have occurred."

You don't want to be like Job. You want to attract good things to yourself by faith in God, like the woman with the issue of blood did in Mark 5. She'd been sick for 12 years and was bankrupt from the many doctor bills. Yet when she heard about Jesus, she believed that if she touched His garment she would become well. And that's what happened.

If that woman could believe God in her situation, think what you can do. You have God's written Word and a New Covenant full of promises that cover every area of your life. As a believer who has devoted your life to Christ, you have nothing to fear—except fear itself.

Of course, you will have to control your thoughts to stay free of fear. Even if you know what the Bible says, you'll have to fight a battle in your mind to stay in faith because the world around you will always be talking fear. In the morning, you may read the assurances in Psalm 91:7 that "a thousand may fall at your side, and ten thousand at your right hand, but it shall not approach you."[186] But in the evening, the news broadcasts on television will be blasting the opposite message. These negative reports can make you question God's protection.

I've heard it said many times, "Your faith ends at the point of a question." So you must guard against the contrary voices of the world. They can cause you to question God's ability to keep His Word on your behalf, and that will stop your faith from working. It will introduce doubts into your mind, and as James 1:6-8 says, "He who doubts is like a wave of the sea driven and tossed by the wind. For let not that man suppose he will receive anything from the Lord; he is a double-minded man, unstable in all his ways."[187]

To keep from being double-minded, sometimes you have to make the conscious decision to turn off the news. You have to close your ears to every other voice that's clamoring for your attention and set your focus on God's promises alone. When you nourish yourself on a steady diet from God's Word, it acts like an anchor for your soul. It prevents your mind, will and emotions from drifting away from God's promises into the strong current of fear.

In any situation, you're either in faith or in fear. So make sure you steer clear of the latter. Ride high above the tide of adversity and make the determination to believe in God's protection without wavering. Adopt the attitude that says, "God said it, so that settles it! Let God be found true, though every man be found a liar!"

Simple Steps to Defeating Fear

I like what the Apostle Paul taught about this. He instructed us to defeat the realm of darkness the moment fear tries to approach by responding with unwavering faith. "Don't be intimidated by your enemies," he said. "This will be a sign to them that they are going to be destroyed, but that you are going to be saved, even by God himself." [188]

That means no matter what hits you, never allow yourself to act shaken by it. Instead, remain calm and collected. Act as if the King of the Universe was handling the situation—because He is. Your refusal to show any sign of distress or concern will be evidence to the enemy that his defeat is imminent. But if you react with fearful emotions, you become obvious prey to the enemy and will be easy to devour.

First Peter 5:8 warns, "Stay alert! Watch out for your great enemy, the devil. He prowls around like a roaring lion, looking for someone to devour." Notice, it's not God who's your adversary. He's not the one who's giving you problems. Your adversary is the devil. He and he alone is the author of all adversity.

To deal with him wisely, you must be sober and think with a clear head. You can't allow yourself to get emotional or careless and be lulled into a false sense of security. You must always be alert.

Why? Because, as Peter said, the devil is on a never-ending search for someone to destroy. He's always prowling around looking for those he can devour. He can't devour just anyone, only those who are vulnerable. Those who are in rebellion to God, ignorant, or intoxicated with fear.

The devil is not the only one on a never-ending search. God is too. But instead of looking for someone to destroy, He is looking "to show Himself strong on behalf of those whose heart is loyal to Him."[189]

Believe the Word
not Your Natural Reasoning

One of the central themes of the Bible is: *Fear not*. In one form or another God gives us that command over and over. Eighty times when He tells us not to fear, He accompanies that command with promises of protection. He puts the two together because the promises in His Word are what remove fear from our lives.

He said in Proverbs 1:33, "But the one who always listens to me will live undisturbed in a heavenly peace. Free from fear, confident and courageous, you will rest unafraid and sheltered from the storms of life."[190] So the person who chooses to listen to and believe the Lord, rather than the news reports or what man says, will not live with tormenting dread or fear. Instead he'll abide in peace and tranquility, safe and secure from all harm, surrounded by the calm assurance of God's faithful protection.

That's what happened with the Israelites during the last plague Egypt suffered when the firstborn in every household died. God sent the Israelites His Word through Moses. He instructed them to cover their doorposts with blood, they listened, obeyed, and were protected.

It would have been easy for the Hebrews to dismiss the words of Moses. They could have decided he'd lost his mind. After all, nobody had ever put blood over a doorpost for protection in the past. For that matter, nobody had ever heard of a plague that singled out and killed only the firstborn child.

If they'd depended on their own natural reasoning, the Hebrews would have doubted the instructions the Lord had given Moses. They would have ignored God's Word and their firstborn would have perished just like the Egyptians. The same is true for us as believers today. If we let our natural reasoning determine the course we take, we'll be in trouble. We'll miss out on God's plan because our natural mind can't grasp it. For "the mind of the flesh [which is sense and reason without the Holy Spirit] is death."[191]

As I've pointed out throughout this book, listening to and obeying the voice of the Lord is quite often a matter of life and death! But what we choose to do is up to us. The Hebrews chose wisely. They listened to and obeyed the Lord's instruction. So when the death angel came through the land, it passed over every home in Goshen that had blood on its doorpost.

God had promised them in Exodus 12:13, "The blood shall be a sign for you on the houses where you are. And when I see the blood, I will pass over you. And the plague shall not be on you to destroy you when I strike the land of Egypt."[192] And God kept that promise.

He'll do the same for you. When you apply the blood of Jesus over your family and home, "no plague will touch you or destroy you." You have God's promise. You can stand on it. If you cover yourself and your loved ones in the blood of Jesus, danger will pass over you. You and your household will be protected.

A Double Portion of Peace

The key though is remaining resolute in mind. As Isaiah 26:3 says, God "will keep in perfect peace all those who trust in him, whose thoughts turn often to the Lord."[193] Notice that doesn't guarantee God will keep those who only turn their thoughts toward the Lord when trouble arises. It says that those whose thoughts are *often* turned toward Him will remain in perfect peace. The *New Living Translation* says, "whose thoughts are fixed on you."

The phrase *perfect peace* there in Hebrew is actually *shalom shalom*. It indicates the Lord will give a double portion of peace to those who continue to trust and meditate on Him.

What direction are your thoughts turned? What do you allow yourself to think about? What do you fear? Economic disaster? Flying? Chemical warfare? Shootings?

When you find your thoughts being turned toward fear, you can turn them around by simply saying out loud what the Word of God says: "I will not fear the terror by night. A thousand may fall at my side and ten thousand at my right hand, but it shall not come near me." You can strengthen your faith by declaring the protective promises of God.

Remember, the Bible says:

- If God is for us, who is against us?[194]

- In all these things we overwhelmingly conquer through Him who loved us.[195]

- Take courage, fear not. Behold, your God will come with vengeance; the recompense of God will come, but He will save you. [196]

- Their circumstances will never shake them and others will never forget their example. They will not live in fear or dread of what may come, for their hearts are firm, ever secure in their faith. Steady and strong, they will not be afraid, but will calmly face their every foe until they go down in defeat.[197]

With promises like that you and I have every reason to be confident that God will take care of us no matter what the world around us is experiencing. We don't have to give fear any place at all in our lives. If we'll listen to and believe God's Word, we truly can *fear not*!

Our Covenant with God promises protection no matter how dangerous it gets out here!

PROTECTION CONFESSION

Heavenly Father, I declare that You alone are my refuge and my place of safety. I put my trust in You to keep me safe from all harm. I live a calm and peaceful life because I dwell under the protective umbrella of the Almighty.

You rescue me from every trap and snare set by the enemy. I declare all his plots and plans are aborted and come to naught, in Jesus Name. Your faithful promises are my armor and protection.

You hold me safe, beyond the reach of my enemies and keep me from violent opponents. I am the God-begotten, therefore, I am the God-protected and the evil one can't lay a hand on me! Your Word builds a hedge of protection around me.

You are my hiding place and surround me with songs of deliverance. No weapon that is formed against me shall prosper and every tongue that rises against me shall be proven wrong. This is my heritage in the Lord.

You have given me authority over all the powers of darkness and whatever I forbid on earth is what's forbidden in Heaven. I forbid evil and calamity to come near my dwelling. I command the angels of God to mount a garrison about me and protect me from all harm. Because I belong to Christ, I am delivered from the curse and the Blessing of God rests on me.

I will not give fear any place in my life. I will not fret or become anxious about anything because I trust in the Lord with all my heart. I live undisturbed, free from fear, confident and courageous, unafraid and sheltered from the storms of life.

I diligently guard my heart, listening to and obeying the voice of the Holy Spirit. He leads and guides me, warning me of things to come. The Good Shepherd leads me beside still waters and green pastures.

For I know in Whom I have believed, and I am fully persuaded that He is able to keep and guard what I have entrusted to Him. Surely goodness and mercy shall follow me all the days of my life! I live a long, healthy, satisfied life.

Since God is for me, who can be against me? My heart is fixed on the Lord, steady and strong under the Shadow of the Almighty! I am more than a conqueror in Christ.

SCRIPTURES FOR SUPERNATURAL PROTECTION

The sheer volume of scriptures in the Bible referring to protection is eye opening. Think of this as your inheritance—which it is. You, my friend, are an heir to all the promises of God. This book deals with the subject of protection, but you've inherited so much more.

As you read these verses, remember God's key to success as described in Joshua 1:8, "This book of the law shall not depart from your mouth, but you shall meditate on it day and night, so that you may be careful to do according to all that is written in it; for then you will make your way prosperous, and then you will have success."

Let these truths take root in your heart and flourish in your mouth. Be consistent. Make meditating and speaking God's Words an integral part of your life. As you do, the Word of God will go from letters on a page to seeds flourishing in your heart. The blessings of God will take root and grow in your life. Be blessed and protected.

Protection

1 John 5:18 MSG
The God-begotten are also the God-protected. The Evil One can't lay a hand on them.

2 Thessalonians 3:3 NIV
But the Lord is faithful, and he will strengthen you and protect you from the evil one.

Psalm 7:10 TPT
God, your wrap-around presence is my protection and my defense. You bring victory to all who reach out for you.

Psalm 25:21 TPT
Your perfection and faithfulness are my bodyguards, for you are my hope and I trust in you as my only protection.

Psalm 61:3 TPT
Lord, you are a paradise of protection to me. You lift me high above the fray. None of my foes can touch me when I'm held firmly in your wrap-around presence!

Psalm 71:3 TPT
You're the only place of protection for me. I keep coming back to hide myself in you, for you are like a mountain-cliff fortress where I'm kept safe.

Psalm 89:18 TPT
You are our King, the holiest one of all; your wrap-around presence is our protection.

Proverbs 14:3 TPT
The words of a proud fool will all come back to haunt him. But the words of the wise will become a shield of protection around them.

Proverbs 30:5 TPT
Every promise from the faithful God is pure and proves to be true. He is a wrap-around shield of protection for all his lovers who run to hide in him.

Psalm 17:8 TPT
Protect me from harm; keep an eye on me like you would a child reflected in the twinkling of your eye. Yes, hide me within the shelter of your embrace, under your outstretched wings.

Psalm 28:9 TPT
Keep protecting and cherishing your chosen ones; in you they will never fall. Like a shepherd going before us, keep leading us forward, forever carrying us in your arms!

Psalm 31:21 TPT
The name of the Lord is blessed and lifted high! For his marvelous miracle of mercy protected me when I was over-whelmed by my enemies.

Psalm 31:23 TPT
The Lord protects and preserves all those who are loyal to him. But he pays back in full all those who reject him in their pride.

Psalm 34:20 TPT
God will be your bodyguard to protect you when trouble is near. Not one bone will be broken.

Psalm 35:2-3 TPT
Put on your armor, Lord; take up your shield and protect me. Rise up, mighty God! Grab your weapons of war and block the way of the wicked who come to fight me. Stand for me when they stand against me! Speak over my soul: "I am your strong Savior!"

Psalm 35:10 TPT
Everything inside of me will shout it out: "There's no one like you, Lord!" For look at how you protect the weak and helpless from the strong and heartless who oppress them.

Psalm 41:2 TPT
The Lord will preserve and protect them. They'll be honored and esteemed while their enemies are defeated.

Psalm 59:1 TPT
My God, protect me! Keep me safe from all my enemies, for they're coming to kill me. Put me in a high place out of their reach—a place so high that these assassins will never find me.

Psalm 62:2 TPT
He alone is my safe place; his wrap-around presence always protects me. For he is my champion defender; there's no risk of failure with God. So why would I let worry paralyze me, even when troubles multiply around me?

Psalm 73:26 TPT
When I trust in you, I have a strong and glorious presence protecting and anointing me. Forever you're all I need!

Psalm 91:3 TPT
He will rescue you from every hidden trap of the enemy, and he will protect you from false accusation and any deadly curse.

Psalm 91:4 TPT
His massive arms are wrapped around you, protecting you. You can run under his covering of majesty and hide. His arms of faithfulness are a shield keeping you from harm.

Psalm 91:14 TPT
For here is what the Lord has spoken to me: "Because you have delighted in me as my great lover, I will greatly protect you. I will set you in a high place, safe and secure before my face.

Psalm 102:28 TPT
Generation after generation our descendants will live securely, for you are the one protecting us, keeping us for yourself.

Psalm 121:6 TPT
He's protecting you from all danger both day and night.

Psalm 121:8 TPT
You will be guarded by God himself. You will be safe when you leave your home and safely you will return. He will protect you now, and he'll protect you forevermore!

Psalm 141:9-10 TPT
Protect me! Keep me from the traps of wickedness they set for me. Let them all stumble into their own traps while I escape without a scratch!

Proverbs 2:8 TPT
He becomes your personal bodyguard as you follow his ways, protecting and guarding you as you choose what is right.

Proverbs 2:11 TPT
If you choose to follow good counsel, divine design will watch over you and understanding will protect you from making poor choices.

Proverbs 4:6 TPT
Stick with wisdom and she will stick to you, protecting you throughout your days. She will rescue all those who passionately listen to her voice.

Proverbs 23:11 TPT
For they have a mighty protector, a loving redeemer, who watches over them, and he will stand up for their cause.

Isaiah 25:4 TPT
You have been a fortress-protector for the poor, a mighty stronghold for the needy in their distress, a shelter from the sudden storm, and a shade from the shimmering heat of the day.

Isaiah 49:2 TPT

He gives me words that pierce and penetrate. He hid me and protected me in the shadow of his hand. He prepared me like a polished arrow and concealed me in his quiver.

Mark 16:18 TPT

They will be supernaturally protected from snakes and from drinking anything poisonous. And they will lay hands on the sick and heal them."

John 17:11 TPT

"Holy Father...I ask that by the power of your name, protect each one that you have given me, and watch over them so that they will be united as one, even as we are one.

Ephesians 6:11 TPT

Put on God's complete set of armor provided for you, so that you will be protected as you fight against the evil strategies of the accuser!

Ephesians 6:14 TPT

Put on truth as a belt to strengthen you to stand in triumph. Put on holiness as the protective armor that covers your heart.

Ephesians 6:17 TPT

Embrace the power of salvation's full deliverance, like a helmet to protect your thoughts from lies. And take the mighty razor-sharp Spirit-sword of the spoken Word of God.

1 John 5:18 MSG
The God-begotten are also the God-protected. The Evil One can't lay a hand on him.

Help

Psalm 12:5 TPT
But the Lord says, "Now I will arise! I will defend the poor, those who were plundered, the oppressed, and the needy who groan for help. I will arise to rescue and protect them!"

Psalm 121:1-2 NKJV
I will lift up my eyes to the hills—from whence comes my help? My help comes from the Lord, who made heaven and earth.

Psalm 124:7-8 NKJV
Our soul has escaped as a bird from the snare of the fowler; the snare is broken, and we have escaped. Our help is in the name of the Lord, who made heaven and earth.

Psalm 124:7-8 TPT
We are free from the hunter's trap; their snare is broken and we have escaped! For the same God who made everything, our Creator and our mighty maker, he himself is our helper and defender!

Hebrews 13:5-6 NKJV
For He Himself has said, "I will never leave you nor forsake you." So we may boldly say: "The Lord is my helper; I will not fear. What can man do to me?"

Keep

Genesis 28:15 NKJV
Behold, I am with you and will keep you wherever you go...I will not leave you until I have done what I have spoken to you.

Psalm 12:7-8 TPT
Lord, you will keep us forever safe, out of the reach of the wicked. Even though they strut and prowl, tolerating and celebrating what is worthless and vile, you will still lift up those who are yours!

Psalm 16:1 TPT
Keep me safe, O mighty God. I run for dear life to you, my safe place.

Psalm 31:4 NIV
Keep me free from the trap that is set for me, for you are my refuge.

Psalm 140:4 TPT
Keep me safe, Lord, out of reach from these wicked and violent men, and guard me, God, for they have plotted an evil scheme to ruin me and bring me down.

Isaiah 26:3 NKJV
You will keep him in perfect peace, whose mind is stayed on You, because he trusts in You.

John 17:15-16 MSG
I'm not asking that you take them out of the world but that
you guard them from the Evil One. They are no more defined
by the world than I am defined by the world.

Deliver

Nehemiah 9:27 NIV
From heaven you heard them, and in your great compassion
you gave them deliverers, who rescued them from the hand of
their enemies.

Job 22:30 NKJV
He will even deliver one who is not innocent; Yes, he will be
delivered by the purity of your hands.

Psalm 6:4 TPT
Turn to me and deliver my life because I know you love and
desire to have me as your very own.

Psalm 18:6 TPT
I cried out to you in my distress, the delivering God, and from
your temple-throne you heard my troubled cry. My sobs came
right into your heart and you turned your face to rescue me.

Psalm 18:17 NKJV
He delivered me from my strong enemy, from those who hated
me, for they were too strong for me.

Psalm 18:27 TPT
To the humble you bring heaven's deliverance. But the proud and haughty you disregard.

Psalm 20:6 NKJV
I know that the Lord saves His anointed; He will answer him from His holy heaven with the saving strength of His right hand.

Psalm 20:7 TPT
Some find their strength in their weapons and wisdom, but my miracle deliverance can never be won by men. Our boast is in the Lord our God, who makes us strong and gives us victory!

Psalm 22:5 TPT
Every time they cried out to you in their despair, you were faithful to deliver them; you didn't disappoint them.

Psalm 31:3-4 NLT
You are my rock and my fortress. For the honor of your name, lead me out of this danger. Pull me from the trap my enemies set for me, for I find protection in you alone.

Psalm 31:15 TPT
My life, my every moment, my destiny-it's all in your hands. So I know you can deliver me from those who persecute me relentlessly.

Psalm 31:19 NLT
How great is the goodness you have stored up for those who fear you. You lavish it on those who come to you for protection, blessing them before the watching world.

Psalm 34:6 TPT
When I had nothing, desperate and defeated, I cried out to the Lord and he heard me, bringing his miracle-deliverance when I needed it most.

Psalm 35:9 TPT
Then my fears will dissolve into limitless joy; my whole being will overflow with gladness because of your mighty deliverance.

Psalm 37:40 NLT
The Lord helps them, rescuing them from the wicked. He saves them, and they find shelter in him.

Psalm 54:1 NLT
Come with great power, O God, and rescue me! Defend me with your might.

Psalm 107:20 TPT
God spoke the words "Be healed," and we were healed, delivered from death's door!

Psalm 144:7 TPT
Reach down from your heavens and rescue me from this hell, and deliver me from these dark powers.

2 Timothy 4:18 NLT

Yes, and the Lord will deliver me from every evil attack and will bring me safely into his heavenly Kingdom.

Psalm 27:5-6 TPT

In his shelter in the day of trouble, that's where you'll find me, for he hides me there in his holiness. He has smuggled me into his secret place, where I'm kept safe and secure—out of reach from all my enemies.

Psalm 31:3-4 TPT

For you are my high fortress, where I'm kept safe. You are to me a stronghold of salvation. When you deliver me out of this peril, it will bring glory to your name. As you guide me forth I'll be kept safe from the hidden snares of the enemy—the secret traps that lie before me—for you have become my rock of strength.

Psalm 55:18 NLT

He ransoms me and keeps me safe from the battle waged against me, though many still oppose me.

Psalm 61:2-3 NLT

From the ends of the earth, I cry to you for help when my heart is overwhelmed. Lead me to the towering rock of safety, for you are my safe refuge, a fortress where my enemies cannot reach me.

Psalm 91:14 TPT
Because you have delighted in me as my great lover, I will greatly protect you. I will set you in a high place, safe and secure before my face.

Psalm 94:22-23 TPT
But I know that all their evil plans will boomerang back onto them. Every plot they hatch will simply seal their own doom. For you, my God, you will destroy them, giving them what they deserve. For you are my true tower of strength, my safe place, my hideout, and my true shelter.

Psalm 121:7-8 MSG
God guards you from every evil, he guards your very life. He guards you when you leave and when you return, he guards you now, he guards you always.

Psalm 144:1 NLT
He trains my hands for war and gives my fingers skill for battle.

Proverbs 3:24 TPT
You will sleep like a baby, safe and sound—your rest will be sweet and secure.

John 17:12 TPT
While I was with these that you have given me, I have kept them safe by your name that you have given me. Not one of them is lost, except the one that was destined to be lost, so that the Scripture would be fulfilled.

Psalm 66:9 TPT
There's no doubt about it; God holds our lives safely in his hands. He's the one who keeps us faithfully following him.

Psalm 121:5 TPT
Jehovah himself will watch over you; he's always at your side to shelter you safely in his presence.

Psalm 121:8 TPT
You will be guarded by God himself. You will be safe when you leave your home and safely you will return. He will protect you now, and he'll protect you forevermore!

Psalm 28:7 TPT
You are my strength and my shield from every danger. When I fully trust in you, help is on the way. I jump for joy and burst forth with ecstatic, passionate praise! I will sing songs of what you mean to me!

Psalm 56:9 TPT
The very moment I call to you for a father's help the tide of battle turns and my enemies flee. This one thing I know: God is on my side!

Isaiah 41:10 TPT
Do not yield to fear, for I am always near. Never turn your gaze from me, for I am your faithful God. I will infuse you with my strength and help you in every situation. I will hold you firmly with my victorious right hand.'

John 14:18 TPT
I promise that I will never leave you helpless or abandon you as orphans-I will come back to you!

Psalm 18:48 TPT
He rescues me from my enemies; he lifts me up high and keeps me out of reach, far from the grasp of my violent foe.

Angels

Psalm 34:7 NKJV
The angel of the Lord encamps all around those who fear Him, and delivers them.

Psalm 59:11 TPT
Scatter them with your armies of angels, O mighty God, our protector! Use your awesome power to make them wanderers and vagabonds and then bring them down.

Psalm 91:11 TPT
God sends angels with special orders to protect you wherever you go, defending you from all harm.

Psalm 103:20-21 NLT
Praise the Lord, you angels, you mighty ones who carry out his plans, listening for each of his commands. Yes, praise the Lord, you armies of angels who serve him and do his will!

Psalm 104:4 NKJV
Who makes His angels spirits, His ministers a flame of fire

Matthew 4:6 TPT
He will command his angels to protect you and they will lift you up so that you won't even bruise your foot on a rock.

Luke 4:10-11 TPT
For it is written in the Scriptures, 'God has given his angels instructions to protect you from harm. For the hands of angels will hold you up and keep you from hurting even one foot on a stone.'"

Acts 12:11 NLT
The Lord has sent his angel and saved me…from what…was planned for me.

Hebrews 1:14 NLT
Therefore, angels are only servants—spirits sent to care for people who will inherit salvation.

Rescue

2 Samuel 22:18 NLT
He rescued me from my powerful enemies, from those who hated me and were too strong for me.

Job 22:30 NLT
Even sinners will be rescued; they will be rescued because your hands are pure."

Psalm 3:7 NLT
Rescue me, my God! Slap all my enemies in the face! Shatter the teeth of the wicked!

Psalm 7:1 NLT
I come to you for protection, O LORD my God. Save me from my persecutors-rescue me!

Psalm 18:16 TPT
He then reached down from heaven, all the way from the sky to the sea. He reached down into my darkness to rescue me! He took me out of my calamity and chaos and drew me to himself, taking me from the depths of my despair!

Psalm 17:13 NLT
Arise, O LORD! Stand against them, and bring them to their knees! Rescue me from the wicked with your sword!

Psalm 18:17 NLT
He rescued me from my powerful enemies, from those who hated me and were too strong for me.

Psalm 18:48 NLT
You hold me safe beyond the reach of my enemies; you save me from violent opponents.

Psalm 18:48 TPT
He rescues me from my enemies; he lifts me up high and keeps me out of reach, far from the grasp of my violent foe.

Psalm 31:16 NLT
Let your favor shine on your servant. In your unfailing love, rescue me.

Psalm 34:17 NLT
The LORD hears his people when they call to him for help. He rescues them from all their troubles.

Psalm 34:19 NLT
The righteous person faces many troubles, but the LORD comes to the rescue each time.

Psalm 54:7 TPT
Through you I'm saved-rescued from every trouble. I've seen with my eyes the defeat of my enemies. I've triumphed over them all!

Psalm 68:20 NLT
Our God is a God who saves! The Sovereign LORD rescues us from death.

Psalm 103:4 TPT
You've rescued me from hell and saved my life. You've crowned me with love and mercy.

Psalm 116:8 TPT
God has rescued my soul from death's fear and dried my eyes of many tears. He's kept my feet firmly on his path.

Psalm 140:1 NLT
O LORD, rescue me from evil people. Protect me from those who are violent.

Psalm 140:7 NLT
O Sovereign LORD, the strong one who rescued me, you protected me on the day of battle.

Psalm 142:6 NLT
Hear my cry, for I am very low. Rescue me from my persecutors, for they are too strong for me.

Psalm 144:2 NLT
He is my loving ally and my fortress, my tower of safety, my rescuer. He is my shield, and I take refuge in him.

Psalm 144:7 NLT
Reach down from heaven and rescue me; rescue me from deep waters, from the power of my enemies.

Proverbs 11:8 NLT
The godly are rescued from trouble, and it falls on the wicked instead.

Jeremiah 15:21 NKJV
I will deliver you from the hand of the wicked, and I will redeem you from the grip of the terrible.

2 Corinthians 1:10 NLT
And he did rescue us from mortal danger, and he will rescue us again. We have placed our confidence in him, and he will continue to rescue us.

2 Corinthians 1:10 TPT
He has rescued us from terrifying encounters with death. And now we fasten our hopes on him to continue to deliver us from death yet again.

Galatians 3:13 NLT

But Christ has rescued us from the curse pronounced by the law. When he was hung on the cross, he took upon himself the curse for our wrongdoing. For it is written in the Scriptures, "Cursed is everyone who is hung on a tree."

Colossians 1:13 NLT

For he has rescued us from the kingdom of darkness and transferred us into the Kingdom of his dear Son.

Colossians 1:13 TPT

He has rescued us completely from the tyrannical rule of darkness and has translated us into the kingdom realm of his beloved Son.

False Accusations / Vindication

2 Samuel 22:48-49 NLT

He is the God who pays back those who harm me; he brings down the nations under me and delivers me from my enemies. You hold me safe beyond the reach of my enemies; you save me from violent opponents.

Job 5:15 NLT

He rescues the poor from the cutting words of the strong, and rescues them from the clutches of the powerful.

Job 5:21 NLT

You will be safe from slander and have no fear when destruction comes.

Psalm 31:20 TPT
So hide all your beloved ones in the sheltered, secret place before your face. Overshadow them by your glory-presence. Keep them from these accusations, the brutal insults of evil men. Tuck them safely away in the tabernacle where you dwell.

Psalm 43:1 NLT
Declare me innocent, O God! Defend me against these ungodly people. Rescue me from these unjust liars.

Psalm 43:1 TPT
Deliver me from these lying degenerates.

Psalm 120:2 NLT
Rescue me, O LORD, from liars and from all deceitful people.

Psalm 144:11 TPT
Deliver me and save me from these dark powers who speak nothing but lies. Their words are pure deceit and you can't trust anything they say.

Psalm 25:19-20 NLT
See how many enemies I have and how viciously they hate me! Protect me! Rescue my life from them!

Isaiah 54:17 NKJV
No weapon formed against you shall prosper, and every tongue which rises against you in judgment you shall condemn. This is the heritage of the servants of the lord.

Isaiah 54:17 TPT
But I promise you, no weapon meant to hurt you will succeed, and you will refute every accusing word spoken against you. This promise is the inheritance of Yahweh's servants, and their vindication is from me," says Yahweh.

Ephesians 6:13 TPT
Because of this, you must wear all the armor that God provides so you're protected as you confront the slanderer, for you are destined for all things and will rise victorious.

Safety

Psalm 31:2b NLT
Be for me a great rock of safety, a fortress where my enemies cannot reach me.

Psalm 62:2 TPT
He alone is my safe place; his wrap-around presence always protects me. For he is my champion defender; there's no risk of failure with God. So why would I let worry paralyze me, even when troubles multiply around me?

Proverbs 1:33 NKJV
But whoever listens to me will dwell safely, and will be secure without fear of evil.

Zechariah 10:11 NLT
They will pass safely through the sea of distress, for the waves of the sea will be held back, and the waters…will dry up.

Surround

Psalm 3:5-6 NLT
I lay down and slept, yet I woke up in safety, for the LORD was watching over me. I am not afraid of ten thousand enemies who surround me on every side

Psalm 27:1 TPT
The Lord is my revelation-light to guide me along the way; he's the source of my salvation to defend me every day. I fear no one! I'll never turn back and run from you, Lord; surround and protect me.

Psalm 32:7 TPT
Lord, you are my secret hiding place, protecting me from these troubles, surrounding me with songs of gladness! Your joyous shouts of rescue release my breakthrough.

Psalm 125:2 TPT
Just as the mountains surround Jerusalem, so the Lord's wraparound presence surrounds his people, protecting them now and forever.

Psalm 34:7 NLT
For the angel of the LORD is a guard; he surrounds and defends all who fear him.

Psalm 118:11 NLT
Yes, they surrounded and attacked me, but I destroyed them all with the authority of the LORD.

Shelter / Refuge

2 Samuel 22:3 NLT
My God is my rock, in whom I find protection. He is my shield, the power that saves me, and my place of safety. He is my refuge, my savior, the one who saves me from violence.

Psalm 9:9 NLT
The LORD is a shelter for the oppressed, a refuge in times of trouble.

Psalm 18:2-3 NIV
The Lord is my rock, my fortress and my deliverer; my God is my rock, in whom I take refuge, my shield and the horn of my salvation, my stronghold.

Psalm 31:2-3 NIV
Turn your ear to me, come quickly to my rescue; be my rock of refuge, a strong fortress to save me. Since you are my rock and my fortress, for the sake of your name lead and guide me.

Psalm 36:7 NLT
How precious is your unfailing love, O God! All humanity finds shelter in the shadow of your wings.

Psalm 61:3 NLT
For you are my safe refuge, a fortress where my enemies cannot reach me.

Psalm 62:7 NLT
My victory and honor come from God alone. He is my refuge, a rock where no enemy can reach me.

Psalm 91:2 NLT
This I declare about the LORD: He alone is my refuge, my place of safety; he is my God, and I trust him.

Psalm 119:114 NLT
You are my refuge and my shield; your word is my source of hope.

Psalm 121:7-8 NKJV
The Lord shall preserve you from all evil; He shall preserve your soul. The Lord shall preserve your going out and your coming in from this time forth, and even forevermore.

Psalm 143:9 NKJV
Deliver me, O LORD, from my enemies; In You I take shelter.

Psalm 144:2 NLT
He is my loving ally and my fortress, my tower of safety, my rescuer. He is my shield, and I take refuge in him. He makes the nations submit to me.

Save

Deuteronomy 20:4 NKJV
For the Lord your God is He who goes with you, to fight for you against your enemies, to save you.

Deuteronomy 33:29 NLT
How blessed you are, O Israel! Who else is like you, a people saved by the Lord? He is your protecting shield and your

triumphant sword! Your enemies will cringe before you, and you will stomp on their backs!

2 Samuel 22:2-4 NLT
The Lord is my rock, my fortress, and my savior; my God is my rock, in whom I find protection. He is my shield, the power that saves me, and my place of safety. He is my refuge, my savior, the one who saves me from violence. I called on the Lord, who is worthy of praise, and he saved me from my enemies.

Psalm 7:1 NLT
I come to you for protection, O LORD my God. Save me from my persecutors-rescue me!

Psalm 18:2 NLT
The LORD is my rock, my fortress, and my savior; my God is my rock, in whom I find protection. He is my shield, the power that saves me, and my place of safety.

Psalm 18:3 NLT
I called on the LORD, who is worthy of praise, and he saved me from my enemies.

Psalm 20:6 NKJV
Now I know that the LORD saves His anointed; He will answer him from His holy heaven with the saving strength of His right hand.

Psalm 28:8 TPT
You will be the inner strength of all your people, the mighty protector of all, the saving strength for all your anointed ones.

Psalm 44:7 NKJV
But You have saved us from our enemies, and have put to shame those who hated us.

Daniel 6:27 NLT
He rescues and saves his people; he performs miraculous signs and wonders in the heavens and on earth. He has rescued Daniel from the power of the lions.

Acts 16:31 NLT
Believe in the Lord Jesus and you will be saved, along with everyone in your household.

Romans 10:9-10 NLT
If you openly declare that Jesus is Lord and believe in your heart that God raised him from the dead, you will be saved. For it is by believing in your heart that you are made right with God, and it is by openly declaring your faith that you are saved.

Romans 10:13 NLT
Everyone who calls on the name of the LORD will be saved.

Philippians 1:28 NLT
Don't be intimidated in any way by your enemies. This will be a sign to them that they are going to be destroyed, but that you are going to be saved, even by God himself.

ENDNOTES

[1] (v. 1, NKJV.)
[2] (v. 1, NKJV, 2-5, NIV.)
[3] (1 Sam. 17: 45-47 NIV, *emphasis mine.*)
[4] (Heb. 8:6.)
[5] (Gen. 12:3.)
[6] (2 Cor. 4:18).
[7] (Matt. 17:20.)
[8] (KJV).
[9] (Matt. 28:18, NKJV).
[10] (Phil. 2:9-10).
[11] (Acts 3:6 TPT).
[12] (Matt. 8:8-9).
[13] (v. 10).
[14] (2 Cor. 4:13, TPT).
[15] (MSG).
[16] (Jn. 16:33).
[17] (vs. 1-2, NKJV).
[18] (NKJV).
[19] (2 Kings 6:15).
[20] (vs. 16-18).
[21] (NKJV).
[22] (1 Chron. 16:9).
[23] (Ps. 105:37, KJV).
[24] (KJV).
[25] (KJV).
[26] (NKJV).
[27] (NKJV).
[28] (NKJV).
[29] (AMPC).
[30] (Acts 27:22-26, NKJV).
[31] (KJV).
[32] (NKJV).

[33] (NKJV).
[34] (Is. 54:17 AMPC)
[35] (NKJV).
[36] (NKJV).
[37] (Mk. 11:22)
[38] (Jn. 17:16, MSG).
[39] (Jn. 17:14, MSG).
[40] (Jn. 16:33).
[41] (Job 1:10, NLT, MSG).
[42] (v. 11, MSG).
[43] (Job 3:25).
[44] (KJV).
[45] (Is 5:5).
[46] (Lk. 10:19).
[47] (Col. 1:12-13, NKJV, emphasis mine).
[48] (See Matt. 28:18, Eph. 4:8; Col 2:15.)
[49] (Phil. 2:10).
[50] (Js. 3:15. NKJV).
[51] (Jn. 14:12).
[52] (Phillips).
[53] (NKJV).
[54] (NKJV).
[55] (NKJV).
[56] (v. 6).
[57] (Rom. 2:4).
[58] (NKJV).
[59] (Ps. 31:19).
[60] (Jer. 29:11).
[61] (Ps. 27:13, NASB).
[62] (NKJV).
[63] (v. 19).
[64] (2 Pet. 1:4).
[65] (NKJV).
[66] (AMPC).
[67] (Mk. 4:35-39, KJV).
[68] (TLB).
[69] (vs. 3-4, 14, NKJV).

70 (Ps. 20:6, NKJV).
71 (Ps. 140:12, NKJV).
72 (Ps. 56:9, NKJV).
73 (Ps. 9:10, NKJV).
74 (NKJV)
75 (AMPC).
76 (Eph. 1:17-18, ESV).
77 (v. 12).
78 (vs. 15-16).
79 (Ps. 103:20, NKJV).
80 (KJV).
81 (vs. 9-12, NKJV).
82 (Jn. 16:15, AMPC).
83 (Acts 1:6).
84 (Acts 2:38-39, NKJV).
85 (NASB).
86 (Matt. 13:11, NASB).
87 Names have been changed.
88 (ASV *emphasis mine*).
89 (Jos.10:12-13).   '
90 (vs. 16-17).
91 (vs. 21-22).
92 (Ps. 31:19).
93 (Job 22:30, NASU).
94 (v. 6).
95 (vs. 18-19).
96 (Gen. 18:24, 26).
97 (Gen.19:12-13).
98 (v. 22).
99 (Gal. 3:14).
100 (NIV).
101 (Josh. 2:12-13).
102 (Josh. 6:17).
103 (Josh. 6:23).
104 (NKJV).
105 (NKJV).
106 (Jn. 10:9. NKJV).

[107] (vs. 1-13).
[108] (Ps. 68:19, NKJV).
[109] (Gen. 1:28, KJV).
[110] (Ps. 31:19).
[111] (vs. 3-9 NKJV).
[112] (vs. 14-20 NKJV).
[113] (vs. 12-16 NKJV).
[114] (Gen. 12:1-3, NKJV).
[115] (NKJV).
[116] (NKJV).
[117] (Gen. 26:1-3).
[118] (vs. 12-14).
[119] (2 Sam. 12:7-8, NKJV).
[120] (Jn. 2:5, 7-11).
[121] (NKJV).
[122] (2 Tim. 1:12).
[123] (vs. 37-39, NIV).
[124] (Rom. 4:18).
[125] (KJV).
[126] (Lk. 1:35, 37, NKJV).
[127] (Matt. 9:28-29).
[128] (Matt. 17:20).
[129] (NKJV).
[130] (1 Pet. 5:7).
[131] (Jn. 17:11, 15).
[132] (NIV).
[133] (Gal. 1:4, KJV).
[134] (1 Chron. 4:10).
[135] (MSG).
[136] Names have been changed.
[137] (Is. 54:17, NASB).
[138] (Ps. 57:2. NIV).
[139] (Rom. 3:4, TPT).
[140] (Ps. 56:5-9, TLB).
[141] (Ps. 141:9-10).
[142] (Ps. 140:9-1,3, NASB).
[143] (vs. 4-5, 14-16).

144 (1 Pet. 2:23).
145 (2 Sam. 15:4).
146 (vs. 12-13, 21).
147 (2 Sam. 17:23).
148 (Esth. 3:8-11).
149 (5:6, MSG).
150 (6:7-9, NIV).
151 (NIV).
152 (2 Cor. 10:4, NKJV).
153 (KJV).
154 (NKJV).
155 (KJV, emphasis mine).
156 (Matt. 5:29, NKJV).
157 (Lk. 10:41,42, MSG).
158 (2 Cor. 1:10, NIV).
159 (Is. 10:27, KJV).
160 (Mk. 6:2-3).
161 (v. 5).
162 (1 Sam. 17:28).
163 (v. 29).
164 (v. 37).
165 (v. 22, TLB).
166 (v. 23).
167 (Pro. 4:23).
168 (Lk. 4:28-30).
169 (Jn. 5:41).
170 (Jn. 8:28).
171 (Is. 53:3).
172 (Matt. 22:15).
173 (Jn. 14:30, NIV).
174 (NKJV).
175 (BBE).
176 (Ps. 141:3 NIV)
177 (Lk. 11:53-54).
178 (vs. 5-6).
179 (Gal. 5:16, NKJV).
180 (NKJV).

181 (AMPC).
182 (Ps. 119:143).
183 (Jn. 16:33, NKJV)
184 (NKJV).
185 (Job 3:25).
186 (NKJV).
187 (NKJV).
188 (Phil. 1:28).
189 (2 Chron. 16:9, NKJV).
190 (TPT).
191 (Rom. 8:6, AMPC).
192 (NKJV).
193 (TLB).
194 (Rom. 8:31, NKJV)
195 (Rom. 8:37, NASB).
196 (Is. 35:4, NASB).
197 (Ps. 112:6-8, TPT).

ABOUT THE AUTHOR

 Vikki Burke and her husband, Dennis, founded Dennis Burke Ministries more than 40 years ago. Vikki ministers in churches, women's conferences and seminars with a commitment to see people raised to a higher level of living through the Word of God.

Vikki is the author of numerous CD's and books including: *Some Days You Dance* and *Destiny Held Hostage*.

Vikki's daily devotional, *Enriching Life Daily*, along with other correspondence is personally touching people worldwide. For more information on Vikki:

visit www.dennisburkeministries.org.